KEEP QUIT!

KEEP QUIT!

A Motivational Guide to a Life Without Smoking

Terry A. Rustin, M.D.

 HAZELDEN®

INFORMATION & EDUCATIONAL SERVICES

Hazelden
Center City, Minnesota 55012-0176

06 05 04 03 02 11 10 09 08 07

Library of Congress Cataloging-in-Publication Data
Rustin, Terry A.
   Keep quit : a motivational guide to a life without smoking/
Terry A. Rustin.
      p. cm.
   Includes bibliographical references and index.
   ISBN 1-56838-104-2
   1. Tobacco habit—Relapse—Prevention. I. Title.
RC567.R88 1996
613.85—dc20   95-52662
                                                           CIP

Dedicated to the memory of my mother,
Jean Moss Rustin,
who taught kindness by her example.

Acknowledgments

During the twenty-four years I have worked in the addictions field, I have benefited from the knowledge and experience of hundreds of colleagues. Those with a special interest in nicotine and tobacco dependence have been by far the most eager and dedicated of all. For their support over the years, I especially want to thank Richard Hurt, John Slade, Andrea Barthwell, John Hughes, Paul Earley, Abby Hoffman, Jeff Goldsmith, Lucy Barry Robe, Ken Roy, and the staff of the American Society of Addiction Medicine in Washington and New York.

The inspiration for my approach to relapse prevention derives in large part from the work of James Prochaska and Carlo DiClemente, who developed the Stages of Change model, and William Miller, who developed the motivational counseling approach to therapy. I am also indebted to the work done on the prevention of relapse in addictions other than nicotine and tobacco by Terence Gorski, Arnold Washton, and many others. Without the support and encouragement of the staff of the Addiction Treatment Unit of the Harris County Psychiatric Center in Houston, Texas, this work would never have been completed. Our unit has pioneered the integration of nicotine and tobacco dependence treatment with the treatment of other addictions, and many of the strategies in this book were developed there. No one gave up, in spite of the difficulties. I am proud of the work of this staff and grateful for their efforts.

This book didn't just happen, of course. It arrived after four long, painful, and exhilarating years of growth and maturation, constantly nurtured by my editor, Tim McIndoo. On days when I thought I would never complete it, I lived for Tim's comments in the margins of the early drafts—Yes, he liked it! Three asterisks meant I was really onto something. Every author should have an editor who cares as deeply for the work as does Tim.

While I was working on *Keep Quit!* I know I was often hard to live with (and at most other times, too, to be completely candid). I would often disappear for many hours, losing track of time entirely. I am grateful for my wife, Laura, and my daughter, Rachel, for tolerating my bizarre schedule. Laura, an indexer by profession, agreed to index the text, even though the two of us hardly ever agree about anything. She probably regretted that decision the moment she made it, but she saw the project through. Fortunately for you, she hardly ever took my advice in preparing the index. As you will see, it is clear and precise, and will guide you quickly to the topics you seek. Many thanks, Laura.

Finally, I want to acknowledge the contributions made to this book by the many clients and patients I have had the honor to work with over the years. They have taught me what works; my goal has been to put those successful strategies into this book.

Introduction

The goal of *Keep Quit!* is to help you stay clean and free—to never smoke a cigarette again.

For many years, I have been working on bringing an effective, inexpensive method of recovery from nicotine and tobacco dependence directly to the people who need it; this program is the result. Research has shown that people do better when they move at their own pace, when they set their own goals, and when they take personal responsibility for their recovery. I designed this program with those facts in mind.

Most likely, you have tried to quit smoking before; nearly half of all smokers have, and most of them have tried many times. Why do smokers try to quit, but fail? Every smoker knows someone who says, "Sure, I used to smoke. One day, I decided to quit; tossed those coffin nails away and never smoked again. No problem at all." Makes you want to strangle him. (Or her—but more likely *him*. Women smokers have more difficulty quitting than men smokers do.) Smokers who could quit easily and without help have already done so. There are smokers who can quit by just using the nicotine patch or nicotine gum, or by attending half a dozen classes, or by being hypnotized—but they have already quit. You are still smoking because your dependence is much stronger.

I am using the word "dependence" in the same way we use it when describing an alcoholic as "alcohol dependent" and a cocaine addict as "cocaine dependent." I am a medical doctor, a psychotherapist, and an addictions specialist; I have worked in the addictions treatment field for more than twenty-three years. I discovered long ago that most people who smoke daily meet the criteria for dependence on nicotine (the addicting drug in cigarettes) in the same way that heroin addicts are dependent on heroin and amphetamine addicts are dependent on amphetamines. But there is more:

- Smokers are dependent on the pleasures of smoking—the fire, the smoke, the inhaling, and the exhaling.
- Smokers are dependent on the image of being a smoker (created by cigarette advertising).
- Smokers are dependent on the rituals associated with smoking (the special ways smokers hold, handle, and manipulate their cigarettes).
- Smokers are dependent on the act of smoking, with its smoke, fire, and oral satisfaction.
- Smokers are controlled by the many activities they associate with smoking (eating, drinking alcohol, drinking coffee, having sex, driving a car, and talking on the phone, to name just a few).
- Smokers use nicotine to help them deal with uncomfortable feelings (like anger, embarrassment, fear, depression, loneliness, and boredom, to name a few).
- When smokers try to quit, they experience significant nicotine withdrawal symptoms (such as anxiety, irritability, difficulty concentrating, trouble sleeping, and intense craving for a cigarette).

No wonder it's so hard to quit! Smoking is rewarding, satisfying, and a good deal cheaper than most other addictions. Most of the problems from smoking don't occur until people are past age sixty, and smoking rarely causes any serious social problems. In fact, most smokers find many more reasons to *keep* smoking than to quit smoking.

Over the years, I have tried all sorts of ways to help smokers quit smoking. Most of them didn't work at all. Lectures and advice didn't work; pleading and scolding didn't work; showing pictures of diseased lungs didn't work. So far, I have found only three things that work, each to some degree. They are

- Having a serious heart attack
- Wearing the nicotine patch
- Helping people develop their own plan for quitting smoking

The heart attack method works about 30 percent of the time. You would think that any smoker who has had such a serious medical complication from smoking would quit, but most are not able to—even if they really want to. Breaking free of nicotine and tobacco dependence can be extremely difficult.

Treatment with the nicotine patch doubles the effectiveness of whatever other measures a person is using. Many smokers hesitate to use the patch because of the cost—a full course of patch treatment usually costs between $30 and $300. Each patch costs about $3—about the same as the average smoker spends on cigarettes each day. If you think the patch could help you, consider the expense as an investment in your future.

The very best treatment for dependence on nicotine and tobacco is helping smokers develop their own plan for quitting smoking. You are a unique person; your history, your goals, and your strengths and weaknesses are not the same as any other person's. Personalizing your recovery program will give you the best chance of staying clean and free.

Here are some tools you can use:

- *Quit and Stay Quit:* If you are just thinking about quitting smoking but have not yet made up your mind, you aren't ready for *Keep Quit!* yet. My earlier book, *Quit and Stay Quit,** will help you make a decision. If you would prefer a workbook with similar material, the *Clean and Free* workbooks might suit you better.

- *Countdown to Quit Cards:* If you do better with a structured approach, you may prefer using the *Countdown to Quit Cards.* To use the cards, choose a Quit Day thirty days in the future. Then start on the first card, reading one card each day and answering its questions. Keep one or more cards with you during the day and refer to them often. Some people keep them next to their pack of cigarettes. Each day go on to the next card, so that in thirty days, you reach your Quit Day.

- *Keep Quit!* The book you are reading is designed to take you through your first three hundred days of recovery and beyond. Each page includes information about nicotine and tobacco dependence, followed by some questions and then a suggestion or two. Start with the first page on your Quit Day; read the material and answer the questions. The following day, go on to the next page.

- *Keep Quit! medallion:* Hazelden has designed a special bronze medallion (some people call it a chip) to go with *Keep Quit!* Several of the exercises in this book ask readers to use the chip. I suggest that newly recovering smokers keep their medallion with them at all times to help them stay focused on their goal—staying clean and free.

- Journal: Keep a daily journal to record your thoughts and feelings, the answers to the questions in the book, and notes about your recovery plans. In future years, you will be able

---

*You can order *Quit and Stay Quit,* the *Clean and Free* workbooks, the *Countdown to Quit Cards,* and the *Keep Quit!* medallion from Hazelden Publishing by calling 1-800-328-9000.

to refer to your journal as a chronicle of your recovery, and it will give you strength during times of stress. Choose a well-made notebook for your journal, since it will get a lot of use. When your first journal is filled up, be sure to start another one.

The Stages of Change

You can't make a change until you are *ready* to change. Sometimes, the "getting ready" takes a long time. Let's look at this process of changing.

A year after you started smoking, you probably didn't think you needed to quit. Young smokers often say:

- "Cancer and emphysema are a long way off."
- "Most of my friends smoke."
- "Smoking makes me feel older and more mature."
- "My parents smoke and they don't care if I do."
- "My parents don't smoke and they *don't* want me to."
- "Smoking is a cheap buzz."
- "Who cares?"

Were some of these *your* reasons for smoking when you were young?

As the years passed and you matured, quitting became more important. You became more responsible. You didn't have the endurance you once had. Many of your friends quit smoking. Your doctor advised you to quit. And gradually, you began to consider quitting smoking.

Consider, yes; quit, no. You were thinking about it, wondering about it, maybe even asking for information about it—but you weren't ready to quit just yet.

That first stage, where smokers refuse to quit or don't see any need to quit, is called the "Precontemplation Stage." The second stage, where they think about quitting but aren't quite ready, is called the "Contemplation Stage." About 40 percent of all smokers are in each of these two stages at any time. The other 20 percent have decided to quit; they are in the "Preparation Stage."

Which stage are you in today? If you are in the Precontemplation Stage but know you need to quit "some day," *Quit and Stay Quit* or the first *Clean and Free* workbook ("Get Ready") can help you make progress. Few people in Precontemplation will read this far, so you probably aren't in that stage.

People in Contemplation are ambivalent; they want to quit, and they don't want to quit. They know they'd be better off if they quit, but they don't feel ready. They anticipate failing and expect to suffer, so they hesitate. They want to be convinced (sort of), but they also wish people would leave them alone.

Are you in the Contemplation Stage? If you are barely past Precontemplation, *Quit and Stay Quit* or the second *Clean and Free* workbook ("Get Set") will help you make faster progress. If you are further along than that, the information in the next section, "Getting Ready to Get Ready," will help you move ahead.

People in the Preparation Stage have resolved their ambivalence about quitting. They are ready to quit; they want suggestions and solutions to their problems. They're ready to go.

Are you in the Preparation Stage? If you are, you can find helpful information in *Quit and Stay Quit,* in the third *Clean and Free* workbook ("Go"), or in the *Countdown to Quit Cards.*

Getting Ready to Get Ready

People have probably been telling you that you need to quit smoking for some time. In your life, how many different people have advised you or told you to quit smoking? Most smokers say "hundreds," and name their relatives and family members, their friends, their co-workers, their doctor, and the surgeon general. Who are some of the people that come to your mind?

Over the years, each of these people (and many others) have given you *their* reasons for quitting smoking. These reasons may or may not have also been *your* reasons. You might quit for someone else's reasons for a little while, but the chances are good that you would start smoking again if they were not your reasons too.

Why did those people want you to quit smoking? Were any of these reasons *your* reasons to quit smoking too?

The problem is that since you have heard these reasons over and over again, you have begun to think that they are your reasons. Some of them make perfect sense; we call these reasons *logical reasons*—such as "To avoid getting lung cancer" or "To save money." These are excellent reasons to quit smoking, but you have known for years that smoking causes lung cancer and that it costs you money. These logical reasons were not enough to get you to quit smoking, because they were not *personal reasons*. You will only be able to quit smoking and recover from your dependence on nicotine and tobacco when you are doing it for your own, very personal reasons.

Take a few moments to answer these questions:

- How would you be better off if you quit smoking?
- If you quit smoking, you might live an extra ten years; what would you want to do with those years?
- What sort of impression do you want to make on the people you love?
- What kind of person are you? What kind of person do you want to *become?*

- What would you be able to accomplish as a nonsmoker that you cannot accomplish as a smoker?
- Would you like yourself better if you could quit smoking?
- Besides quitting smoking, what other changes do you want to make in your life?

Are you willing to ask yourself these questions?

Another thing that smokers must deal with is how much they enjoy smoking. Tobacco contains nicotine, a stimulant drug much like cocaine; smokers deliver a dose of nicotine to their brains within ten seconds of inhaling cigarette smoke. But the pleasure of smoking includes more than just the nicotine. Smokers enjoy holding and handling their cigarettes; they like the fire and the smoke; they like having something to concentrate on. Smokers also respond to the image of being a smoker, and the image of being a *Marlboro* smoker, or a *Virginia Slims* smoker, or a *Newport* smoker. Finally, after so many years of smoking, smokers associate a puff of cigarette smoke with hundreds of their daily activities, from getting up to going to bed, and everything in between.

- What do you like about *nicotine?*
- What do you like about the act of *smoking?*
- What do you like about *being a smoker?*
- What things do you *associate with smoking?*

There are so many good things about smoking, it's a wonder anyone ever quits before they die. Smoking can perk you up when you're tired, it can calm you down when you're tense, and it can help you concentrate. It's legal, cheap, and easy to do, and you can buy cigarettes just about anywhere. Why quit?

People quit smoking because there are serious consequences to smoking. Everyone knows that smoking causes lung cancer and heart disease, but there are other kinds of consequences too. Have you thought about them? Take a moment to think about some of the consequences you have already experienced, or consequences that could happen to you.

- Have cigarettes already damaged your body?
- Will cigarettes damage your body if you don't quit smoking?
- Has your smoking hurt or endangered people you love and care about?
- Has your smoking affected your opinion of yourself?

When you have decided that quitting smoking is the most important thing you can do to improve your health and your life, you have moved into the Preparation Stage and you are ready to set a Quit Day.

Setting a Quit Day

Research on people who have successfully quit smoking shows that setting a specific Quit Day and sticking to it is one of the best methods of quitting smoking. In fact, most former smokers have quit in this way.

Decide on which day you intend to quit smoking. It can be any random day or a special day. Some smokers choose a birthday or an anniversary or a holiday. Whichever day you choose, it will become extremely important to you later.

Write down the date of your Quit Day. Circle it on the calendar; tell your friends and family; announce it to your co-workers. Ask for support from everyone you can think of—friends, relatives, your doctor, your recovery group. Pick up some self-help materials, books, or brochures.

If you are the kind of person who functions better with somewhat more structure and organization, you might prefer the

Countdown to Quit Cards. They won't tell you what to do as much as they will guide you to discover your own answers to your problems as you work toward your Quit Day. To use the *Countdown to Quit Cards,* first choose a Quit Day and write the date in your journal. Then, counting your Quit Day as zero, count back thirty days from your Quit Day; this is the day to start on the *Countdown to Quit Cards.* This is the day you will start counting down to your Quit Day, using one card each day. (If you want, you can adjust this a little by devoting two days to a few cards, but experience has shown that working toward a Quit Day about a month away works best.) Start off each day by reading the card for that day and answering the questions. Write down your answers in your journal. Carry the card with you; it fits inside your pocket or even your cigarette pack. When you take out your cigarettes for a smoke, read over the card again.

Just by carrying the cards and starting to think about the future, most smokers cut down by about 25 percent. This makes it much easier to quit when Quit Day rolls around.

Take the questions seriously. These are the same questions I ask my patients in group and individual counseling. Write down your thoughts and feelings in your journal. Do your best to answer each and every question.

Each day, move on to the next card. Continue in this way, counting down to Quit Day. If you are like most people, you will be smoking only a fraction of what you had been smoking by the time you get to your Quit Day, and quitting altogether will be much easier.

On your Quit Day, put away your *Countdown to Quit Cards* and open this book again.

Using Keep Quit! *and Your Journal*

Each page in *Keep Quit!* is designed to give you a few intense minutes of relapse prevention counseling. On your Quit Day, start with the page 23. Read the comments and suggestions, and make some notes in your journal. The following day, go on to the next page. You can carry the book with you or read it at a special time each day. One page a day is plenty; rushing through *Keep Quit!* will lessen your chances of success. (If you make a serious effort, you could easily devote as much time to this program as you once spent smoking—about two hours a day.) I suggest you go through the pages in sequence—their order reflects when certain issues usually arise in early recovery.

Use your journal to record your thoughts and feelings about quitting smoking, your experiences, and yourself. Your journal will soon be filled with valuable information that will help you stay clean and free.

Using the Keep Quit! Medallion

Your medallion, or chip, will be a useful reminder to you of why you decided to quit smoking. In moments of stress, you will find that it gives you something tangible to hold on to. One side says *minute by minute,* reminding you to not let anything distract you from reaching your goal. The other side says *clean and free,* reminding you that by quitting smoking, your body will be cleansed of toxic smoke and chemicals and your spirit will be freed from the control of a destructive addiction. Keep your medallion in your pocket or purse or on a chain around your neck (it fits in the holders designed for displaying silver dollars).

Using the Index

During your first year of recovery, many events will occur that will make you want to smoke again. Most of these issues and situations are discussed somewhere in this book; the index will help you find them. It includes nearly 100 different topics and keywords with references to specific pages in *Keep Quit!* that address these topics. For instance, if you wake up feeling angry and desperately want a cigarette, you can look up *anger* in the index and find page 303, which discusses anger as a relapse issue. Instead of smoking, you could turn to page 303, read it carefully, and answer the questions. By doing this, you will understand yourself better and give yourself a better chance of staying clean and free.

After you have completed the entire book, continue to use the index in the same way. What made you think about smoking *today?* Find an entry that addresses your problem and review it—and always remember to make some notes in your journal.

Medications That Can Help

There is no magic potion that will completely take away your desire to smoke and there is no "Antabuse for tobacco" that would make smoking so distasteful that you would not smoke again. However, a number of medications have been proven helpful; you may choose to ask your doctor to prescribe one of them.

The medications that can help fall into three categories: nicotine replacement products, non-nicotine products that reduce the urge to smoke, and medications that counteract some of the symptoms of withdrawal.

Nicotine Replacement Products

The nicotine gum and the nicotine patch contain pure nicotine (without all the cancer-causing chemicals in tobacco). You absorb the nicotine from the gum through the tissues of your mouth and tongue (not your stomach); you absorb the nicotine from the patch across the skin. The nicotine helps reduce your nicotine withdrawal symptoms (such as irritability, agitation, difficulty concentrating, and mood swings). Withdrawal from nicotine is not pleasant, and these symptoms are often the reason smokers give up their efforts to quit smoking. Many smokers are afraid to quit smoking for fear of having severe withdrawal symptoms.

Research proves that suffering will not help you quit smoking. The nicotine gum and the nicotine patch are safe and effective and can reduce the discomfort of withdrawal.

The nicotine gum (Nicorette) has been available in the United States since 1984, and hundreds of research studies have been done with it. When used as part of a treatment program, it improves the chances for success. When used without any program of recovery, however, it is not very effective.

There are many advantages to the nicotine gum:

- You can control the dose yourself; when you experience nicotine withdrawal symptoms, you can chew a piece of nicotine gum to relieve the symptoms.
- Sucking on a cigarette is part of the satisfaction of smoking; sucking on the gum may be a helpful substitute.
- You can give your system a quick jolt of nicotine to relieve withdrawal symptoms by chewing rapidly, thus raising the nicotine level in your blood very quickly.
- When you are ready to reduce your nicotine dose, you can use the gum to drop down gradually.
- The gum is convenient to carry since it comes in a plastic blister package.

However, there are several disadvantages to nicotine gum:

- There are times when chewing gum is just not possible or acceptable, such as when giving a speech or attending a meeting.
- To reduce your nicotine withdrawal symptoms, you may need as many as twenty-five pieces of gum a day, which can cause pain and soreness in your jaw and neck muscles.
- Because nicotine is not well absorbed from the stomach, you must keep the saliva in your mouth to absorb the nicotine. If you swallow frequently, you will absorb less nicotine and you may get an upset stomach.
- Some people find the gum's taste unpleasant, and they are tempted to chew regular gum with it. Do not do this. Anything that makes your mouth even slightly acidic (coffee, fruit juice, cola, lemon drops, fruit-flavored gum, and so on) prevents the nicotine in the gum from being absorbed.

There are two ways to use the nicotine gum; consider your own situation and decide which is better for you. The standard way is to start with twenty or more pieces of gum each day. The idea is to use enough nicotine to eliminate your craving for a cigarette, and then gradually decrease the number of pieces you use each day over several weeks. In this method, you chew a piece of gum when you feel the urge to smoke (or on a schedule), chewing until you taste the peppery flavor; then park the gum next to your cheek for a while. After thirty minutes, you will have sucked all the nicotine out of that piece.

The alternative way to use the nicotine gum is to use just enough to relieve nicotine withdrawal symptoms when they occur. Half a piece or even a quarter of a piece of gum may be enough. Chew the gum very rapidly to mimic the shot of nicotine a cigarette gives you; as soon as the immediate symptoms are gone (usually in less than two minutes), dispose of the gum.

The other medication available today is the nicotine patch (Habitrol, Nicoderm, ProStep, and Nicotrol). The patches all contain nicotine, but their delivery systems differ and the amount of nicotine in the patches differs, as does the rate at which it is delivered. The patches have been available in the United States since 1991 and there are now dozens of research studies showing that they are effective; use of the nicotine patch approximately doubles the success rate of whatever else you are doing to quit smoking.

The patch offers two main advantages over the gum:

- The patch sends pure nicotine across your skin and into your system at a steady rate all day long. This avoids the swings in nicotine blood levels that contribute to addiction.
- In the morning, you stick a patch on your skin—anywhere it will stick is fine—and forget about it.

Most brands of the nicotine patch come in three different sizes. Which size is right for you? Your answers on the Fagerström Test for Nicotine Dependence will help. This would be a good time to take the test.

Fagerström Test for Nicotine Dependence

Instructions: Answer each of these six questions about your smoking as accurately as possible. Tally the points for each question and add them together; your total score will determine the intensity of your nicotine dependence.

1. How soon after you wake up do you smoke your first cigarette?

within 5 minutes	3 points
5–30 minutes	2 points
31–60 minutes	1 point
after 60 minutes	0 points

2. Is it hard for you to not smoke in places where it is forbidden, such as in church, at the library, in a movie, in court, or in the hospital?

Yes	1 point
No	0 points

3. Which cigarette would you hate most to give up?

The first one in the morning	1 point
Any other one	0 points

4. How many cigarettes do you smoke each day?

10 or fewer	0 points
11–20	1 point

21–30	2 points
31 or more	3 points

5. Do you smoke more during the first hours after waking up than during the rest of the day?

Yes	1 point
No	0 points

6. Do you still smoke if you are so sick that you are in bed most of the day?

Yes	1 point
No	0 points

TOTAL _____ POINTS

(Adapted from Heatherton, T. F. , L. T. Kozlowski, R. C. Frecker, and K. O. Fagerström. 1991. The Fagerström Test for Nicotine Dependence: A revision of the Fagerström Tolerance Questionnaire. *British Journal of Addictions* 86:1119–27.)

If you score 7 to 10 points on the Fagerström Test, your nicotine dependence is high; you should start with the largest patch. If you score 4 to 6 on the Fagerström Test, your nicotine dependence is moderate; start with the middle-sized patch. If you score less than 4 on the Fagerström Test, your nicotine dependence is lower than that of most smokers; you will probably do just fine with the smallest patch, or no patch at all. You and your doctor can decide together when you can drop from one patch to the next smaller size. Some people can do this after one week; others need two months. You should discuss this with your doctor.

The patch has several disadvantages:

- None of the brands of nicotine patch come in more than three doses. Cutting the patch to change the dosage is not a good idea for two reasons: If you cut it, some of the nicotine inside may leak out, and a cut patch does not stick well to the skin.
- Skin reactions to the patch are common; up to half the subjects in some studies had skin irritation from the patch.
- It takes about two hours for the nicotine level in your system to rise after first putting the patch on; therefore, pulling it off at night is not a good idea. When you feel the urge to smoke, rubbing the patch does not help; it is designed to give you a steady dose of nicotine, and not a "rush" like a cigarette does. Some people relapse to smoking in this situation; however, you should not smoke while wearing the patch.

A new form of nicotine delivery, the nicotine inhaler, will be available soon. It sends vaporized nicotine into the lungs where it is quickly absorbed. The nicotine inhaler may be an alternative for smokers who are highly dependent. A nicotine nasal spray is also being studied.

Non-Nicotine Medications That Reduce the Urge to Smoke

Several research studies have shown that clonidine (Catapres) reduces the urge to smoke in many people. Long-term results with clonidine have not been as promising, but it may help some people. Clonidine is available in both tablet form and as a one-week patch.

There are several nonprescription medications (available for years) that are advertised as smoking cessation aids. None of these medications have been proven effective and the FDA has challenged some of them. I do not recommend any of them.

Other Medications That Reduce the Symptoms of Quitting

Buspirone (BuSpar) is a nonaddictive antianxiety medication that may help some people quit smoking by making them less tense. Research results on buspirone are mixed; about half the studies show that it helps and half show that it doesn't. Buspirone is rather expensive, but it is safe.

Sedatives and tranquilizers have been used to reduce the anxiety associated with quitting smoking. Diazepam (Valium), alprazolam (Xanax), chlordiazepoxide (Librium), lorazepam (Ativan), and clorazepate (Tranxene) have all been used. Research does not show that using these medications improves the results in smoking cessation programs. In addition, these medications have addictive properties and must be used only in appropriate situations. I do not recommend using them in smoking cessation programs.

Some antidepressants have been investigated as aids to quitting smoking. Fluoxetine (Prozac) has been shown to reduce or eliminate the weight gain often associated with quitting smoking. Several research studies are currently in progress, looking at whether antidepressant medication would improve the rates of smoking cessation in people with a personal or family history of depression. If you have been seriously depressed in the past, you should discuss this with your doctor right away.

Should you take medication or not? Many smokers have quit with the aid of the patch or the gum, clonidine, or fluoxetine, but many who took medication failed because they put too much faith in the medication alone. Quitting smoking requires hard work; very few people can simply slap on a patch, toss their cigarettes away, and never smoke again. Using this program as your foundation, and the nicotine gum or the nicotine patch to help ease the symptoms of withdrawal, is much more likely to be successful.

If you think medication might help you, discuss it with your doctor. But remember: no medication is going to solve your problems for you—only you can do that.

Other Smoking Cessation Treatments

Many other smoking cessation treatments have come and gone—but a few of them are still in use.

Acupuncture reduces the severity of nicotine withdrawal symptoms for many people. Acupuncture is safe, and if you want to try it, there is no reason not to. Some people report that one treatment was all they needed, others return to the acupuncturist for a series of treatments, and some say it didn't help at all. There is less evidence that staples placed in acupuncture points in the ear or that vitamin injections into these points are helpful.

Hypnotherapy (hypnosis) helps relieve the anxiety of quitting smoking and can help people feel more confident about quitting. When used by qualified therapists as one of their therapy techniques, hypnosis can be very helpful; just being hypnotized, however, does not improve your chances of quitting. Be cautious of stage hypnotists; they are really entertainers, not therapists. Be especially cautious of hypnotists who come to town for a one-day performance and guarantee success.

There are two kinds of *aversive conditioning* in use today. In one kind, some of the pleasurable aspects of smoking (the smoke, the taste, and puffing) are paired with a mild electric shock. In the other, the smoker is told to puff repeatedly until queasy. The goal is to eliminate the pleasurable response smokers have to the sights, smells, and tastes associated with smoking. Many smokers who undergo aversive conditioning subsequently feel nauseated or tense whenever they smell or taste cigarette smoke. However, the aversion tends to wear off fairly quickly, leaving the smoker with no protection against relapse.

From time to time, you may hear about "new medications" or "secret remedies" that claim to take away the desire to smoke. So far, medical research has not found anything that works that well. Some of these "remedies" contain no active medication at all; others contain powerful steroids (like cortisone) that can have serious side effects.

Taking Care of Your Health

Now that you have decided to quit smoking, this would be a good time to see your doctor for a physical, including a chest X ray and an EKG. Hopefully, your exam and your tests will all be negative; quitting smoking now will reduce your chances of becoming ill and dying from the effects of smoking. Cigarettes cause many illnesses: bronchitis, pneumonia, heart disease, emphysema, strokes, and cancer of the lung, breast, colon, head and neck, stomach, and bladder. Each year more than 430,000 Americans and 25,000 Canadians die from diseases caused by smoking. That's the equivalent of three fully loaded jumbo jets crashing and killing everyone on board *every single day*. About 40,000 Americans die each year on the highways; nearly that many die *each month* from smoking. Cigarettes are one of the few products that, when used as directed, kills the user.

When you see your doctor (and even if you don't), this would be a good time to review how you take care of your body. Are you doing the right thing for your health?

- Are you overweight?
- Do you watch the amount of fat and cholesterol you eat?
- Do you exercise regularly?
- Does your drinking ever lead to problems?
- Have you become dependent on alcohol or other drugs?

How would you feel if you quit smoking and then became seriously ill because you didn't take care of yourself in other ways?

Putting It All Together

This program includes all the tools you need to successfully quit smoking and not start again. Only you can provide the most important elements—willingness to accept the challenge and commitment to achieving your goal.

Are you ready to be clean and free?

Keep Quit

Quitting smoking is one of the most important decisions you have ever made. Becoming a nonsmoker is the best thing you can do to improve your health and your future. This book will help you stay clean and free and avoid relapsing. Relapses can be prevented when smokers set *recovery* as their goal instead of setting *quitting* as their goal.

A Step in the Right Direction

This book will help you *keep quit*. You have already stopped smoking. The day you *quit* smoking is _____, which means you have made a commitment to not smoke again. This book will help you fully accept your nicotine and tobacco dependence so that smoking again is simply not an option. Have you truly made a commitment to not start smoking again?

A Suggestion

Begin keeping a journal to record your thoughts and goals during your first months as a nonsmoker. Use a sturdy notebook with enough pages for about a year's worth of entries. Your first activity is to list several good reasons for you to quit smoking. Then take each reason in turn and relate it to three or four specific examples of how you will be better off by not smoking. Tomorrow, continue your progress by reading page 24 in this book. Every day, turn to the next page, read the information, ponder the questions, and use the suggestions to support your recovery.

Working on Recovery Every Day

Most people who try to quit smoking attempt it with no help at all. Only 1 or 2 percent of these people succeed in staying clean and free for a year. Research shows that smokers can improve their chances of keeping quit by getting the support of other people, accepting advice, using the nicotine patch or the nicotine gum, using self-help materials, getting professional counseling, attending meetings of Nicotine Anonymous, and taking positive action every day.

A Step in the Right Direction

Using this book every day will also improve your chances of success.

A Suggestion

Make a commitment to yourself and to your future to work on your recovery every day. Put your commitment in writing in your journal. No one else ever has to see it, but you will know it's there. Are you willing to work on one page of this book *every day?* Each page contains information about nicotine and tobacco dependence, followed by some questions and suggestions. If you just *read* through the book, it will not help you very much; if you *invest* time in responding to the questions and following the suggestions, however, you will greatly improve your chances of success. You already have the book—why not use it?

Three Kinds of Relapse Triggers

No two people are exactly the same, but smokers' relapse triggers tend to fall into a few broad categories. During the first two weeks after quitting, the relapse rate is 50 percent. Most of these relapses are due to one of the following three reasons:

- *Uncomfortable withdrawal symptoms.* Irritability, difficulty concentrating, mood swings, and an intense desire for cigarettes are examples of withdrawal symptoms that recovering smokers sometimes experience.
- *Uncomfortable feelings.* Many recovering smokers used cigarettes to help them deal with anger, frustration, sadness, loneliness, and grief, and they have not yet found other ways of dealing with these feelings.
- *Associations with smoking.* Many recovering smokers find themselves in situations where they previously smoked, and the urge to smoke again becomes overwhelming.

A Step in the Right Direction

How close to relapse did you come today? Did uncomfortable withdrawal symptoms, strong emotions, or associations with smoking bring you close to a relapse?

A Suggestion

Make some notes in your journal about how you plan to deal with each of these three threats to your recovery. What action can you take today?

How Nicotine Is Absorbed

Tobacco smoke contains tiny bits of carbon ("particulate matter"), carbon monoxide and other gases, nicotine, and tar, which is present as microscopic droplets. The tar contains several thousand different chemicals—including benzene, formaldehyde, nitrosamines, and pyrethrins—which cause heart disease, emphysema, and cancer. Nicotine (the chemical that causes addiction) dissolves in the tiny droplets of tar, and the tar carries the nicotine into the lungs. These droplets land on the inside surface of the lungs and are absorbed into the bloodstream—tars and nicotine together. If the smoke is alkaline (as is pipe and cigar smoke), the tars and nicotine can also be absorbed from the surface of the mouth and tongue; if the smoke is acidic (as in cigarette smoke), the tars and nicotine are mainly absorbed from the lungs. It is not surprising, then, that pipe and cigar smokers have high rates of cancer of the mouth, tongue, and lip, while cigarette smokers have high rates of cancer of the lung.

A Step in the Right Direction

Some newly recovering smokers hesitate to use the nicotine patch or the nicotine gum because they contain nicotine. However, these medications contain pure nicotine only, without the more dangerous chemicals found in tobacco, and medical research has shown them to be safe.

A Suggestion

Could these medications help you get through withdrawal?

Make a Clean Break with Smoking

Smokers often have a hard time making a clean break with smoking. They sometimes hang on to a pack or two, or just one or two cigarettes from their last pack. Some justify their actions by saying, "I just want to test myself." Others say, "I don't want to forget how hooked I was; these cigarettes will remind me." And some admit, "I might decide to smoke again." All these people risk relapse by not making a clean break with smoking.

A Step in the Right Direction

Have you hidden a few cigarettes away somewhere? Do you know a place where cigarettes might be, even if you didn't put them there? If so, you may be having trouble making a clean break with smoking. Even if you are no longer smoking, you are leaving yourself at risk for relapse.

A Suggestion

If you have had trouble making a clean break with smoking, today is a good day to begin working on a "Good-bye" letter to tobacco. Start with "Good-bye Tobacco," and tell tobacco why you have decided to leave it behind. Writing a sincere "Good-bye Tobacco" letter, filled with specific details and honest emotions, will help you stay clean and free.

Five Reasons Why People Relapse

Most smokers who try to quit this year will start smoking again. Research shows that 25 percent of people who quit smoking start again in just two days, and that another 25 percent start smoking again within one week. Here are some common reasons why people relapse early on:

- The discomfort of their nicotine withdrawal symptoms was more than they could stand.
- They missed the buzz they got from smoking.
- They missed having a cigarette to handle and suck on.
- They had not learned to deal with stress without smoking.
- They had never made a commitment to staying clean and free in the first place.

A Step in the Right Direction

The fact that you did not smoke today means you have already accomplished more than most people who will try to quit smoking this year. What have you been doing that has helped you? Which of the five relapse issues listed above will be the greatest threat to your recovery?

A Suggestion

Choose one of these five relapse issues that could be a threat to your recovery. Make some notes in your journal about how you have dealt with it so far and what you will do in the months ahead.

The Product Is Nicotine

Cigarette companies are in the business of selling an addictive drug—and they know it. A report written in 1972 by William L. Dunn Jr. of the Philip Morris Company stated:

> *The cigarette should be conceived not as a product but as a package. The product is nicotine. The cigarette is but one of many package layers. . . . The smoke is the final package. The smoker must strip off all these package layers to get at that which he seeks. . . . Think of the cigarette pack as a storage container for a day's supply of nicotine. . . . Think of the cigarette as a dispenser for a dose unit of nicotine. . . . Think of a puff of smoke as the vehicle of nicotine. Smoke is beyond question the most optimized vehicle of nicotine and the cigarette the most optimized dispenser of smoke.*

A Step in the Right Direction

Cigarette companies have been intentionally addicting you to cigarettes since the first day you smoked. How does that make you feel? Were their promotions for cigarettes honest? What can you do about these promotions?

A Suggestion

Write a letter to the president of the tobacco company you have been giving your money to and explain exactly how you feel. You might also want to send a copy of your letter to your local newspaper.

Use Guided Imagery to Relax

Smokers are not necessarily more anxious than nonsmokers, but quitting smoking makes many people tense and anxious. One way of dealing with this anxiety is by using guided imagery—relaxing your body while focusing the power of your mind.

A Step in the Right Direction

Here is a guided imagery exercise you can use; you will find others as you move through this book.

Plan to do this exercise for about five minutes. Sit in a comfortable chair or lie down, legs and arms uncrossed. Close your eyes, and breathe slowly and deeply. With each deep breath, imagine yourself becoming more and more relaxed. Focus on your breathing. Continue to breathe deeply, allowing all the concerns of the day to leave your mind as the air leaves your lungs. When your body is thoroughly relaxed, turn your attention to your lungs, polluted by soot particles from tobacco smoke. Now imagine that with each deep breath, a few of the smoke particles fall off the walls of your lungs, and that with each breath, you blow a few of them out of your body. Continue to breathe deeply and relax. After about five minutes, open your eyes and notice how you feel.

A Suggestion

Use guided imagery every day to help you relax, to deal with stressful situations, and to help focus your mind on recovery.

Everyday Events Can Trigger a Relapse

After years of smoking, smokers associate smoking with dozens of everyday events, such as

- Hearing the telephone ring
- Smelling coffee brewing
- Sitting down to watch TV
- Sitting in a traffic jam
- Lying in bed after having sex

These situations can trigger a chain reaction: the smoker reacts by pulling out a pack of cigarettes, removing one, lighting it, and smoking it—all without any conscious thought.

A Step in the Right Direction

Which everyday events still make you think about smoking? Each of these situations represents a relapse risk for you, because it may trigger the desire to smoke. What are you doing to prevent yourself from relapsing in these situations?

A Suggestion

Make a list of situations that once triggered your automatic smoking. Each day this week, choose one situation from your list and watch for it during that day. When the situation arises, be aware of the changes in your thoughts, feelings, and actions.

The First Two Weeks Are Crucial

Cigarettes give smokers something they can depend on; while life is often unpredictable, cigarettes are always consistent. After not smoking for a period of time, many recovering smokers miss having that one stable thing they can count on. Many recovering smokers miss cigarettes so much that they talk themselves into smoking "just one." Research shows that if recovering smokers take a single puff of a cigarette in the first two weeks after quitting, they have only a 5 percent chance of being smokefree at six months. However, if they can get through the first two weeks without taking a single puff, their chances of being smokefree in six months increase to 40 percent.

A Step in the Right Direction

Have you missed having cigarettes to rely on? Have you hoped that you could smoke "just one"? This is the time to regain control of your thoughts and feelings.

A Suggestion

You can improve your chances of staying clean and free, and regain control of your thinking, by writing a "Good-bye" letter to tobacco. If you have already started one, pull it out, read it over, and add things that you have learned over the last week. If you have not started one, start today. Start with "Good-bye Tobacco," and tell tobacco why you have decided to leave it behind.

Thought Stopping

Many recovering smokers find themselves longing to be able to smoke occasionally without getting hooked again. "Maybe I can just smoke one," they say. "After all, I haven't smoked for quite a while. . . ." This is a dangerous thought. Once a person becomes a regular smoker, that person's brain chemistry is permanently altered. Most recovering smokers who take even a single puff off of a cigarette resume daily smoking. Most of them never get clean and free again.

A Step in the Right Direction

Have you thought about smoking again? Have you had such a thought today? When you have such thoughts (and you probably will have them), you must do something positive to change them. If you allow them to remain in your mind, they will grow and gain strength; it is only a matter of time before they convince you to smoke again.

A Suggestion

You can use a technique called "thought stopping." Practice saying "Stop that!" to yourself the very second that the thought of smoking arises. This simple technique really works, but it requires practice—and it requires that you follow your own advice. Even if this technique does not appeal to you at first, give it a try; after all, what have you got to lose?

Maintaining Your Weight

After quitting smoking, many people replace the constant oral stimulation of smoking with food. This can be a serious problem. Recovering smokers who substitute candy for cigarettes are guaranteed to put on weight: twenty-five M&Ms have 100 calories; eight Hershey's kisses have 210 calories.

A Step in the Right Direction

Here is a list of some good alternatives to high-calorie snacks:

- No-fat pretzels (100 calories in 80 small sticks)
- Air-popped popcorn (70 calories in 3 cups)
- Rice cakes (40 calories per cake)
- Dry Cheerios (80 calories in a cup)
- Cut carrot sticks (100 calories in 20 four-inch sticks)
- Celery (10 calories in a medium stalk)
- Medium apple (90 calories)
- Grapes (80 calories in 25)
- Fat-free saltines (60 calories in 5 crackers)
- Raw bean sprouts (Eat as much as you like)

The Tobacco Companies Manipulated You

The tobacco companies carefully create a specific image of the type of people who smoke each of their brands. One company may market a dozen different brands, all containing similar blends of tobacco and additives. Different brands of cigarettes are made in the same factory, on the same production line—they are even made on the same machines. The only thing that really separates one brand from another is the *image* created by the advertisements. The tobacco companies purposely create different images for their different brands in order to sell as many cigarettes as possible.

A Step in the Right Direction

You did not realize it at the time, but tobacco company promotions manipulated you into choosing a particular brand of cigarettes. The tobacco companies are still trying to influence you through their advertising and promotions. They are not interested in your recovery—they want your money. What can you do to fight back?

A Suggestion

Recall an old ad for the cigarette brand you used to smoke. What caught your attention in that ad? What kind of image did it promote? Why were you attracted to that image? If this image still attracts you, cigarette advertising is a relapse trigger for you.

Tell People You Don't Smoke Anymore

Recovering smokers are often tempted to smoke when someone offers them a cigarette. Some smokers offer cigarettes automatically and unconsciously—smoking is so much a part of their lives that offering a cigarette has become as natural as shaking hands. These smokers mean no harm—they are just so completely addicted to tobacco that they don't realize they have a choice. Recovering smokers know they have a choice; every day, they decide to stay clean and free another day.

A Step in the Right Direction

One day someone may unexpectedly offer you a cigarette, saying, "Here—have one of mine," which sounds like receiving permission to smoke. If this offer catches you off guard, you might accept a cigarette and start smoking again. Could this situation be a relapse trigger for you? How would you answer the person offering you a cigarette?

A Suggestion

Consider saying, "No thanks. Perhaps you didn't know—I don't smoke anymore." Some people will feel guilty or foolish for having offered you a cigarette, but at least they will not do it in the future. What other good responses have you thought of?

Your Relationship with Cigarettes

Smokers develop a special relationship with their cigarettes. It usually begins in adolescence; the average age of starting smoking is about fourteen, and 90 percent of current smokers started before they were twenty. As with most relationships, this one begins with curiosity. Children see adults and other children smoking and wonder what it would be like to smoke. They are clumsy smokers at first, because smoking is not a natural act. As the relationship with cigarettes develops, the beginning smoker gradually learns how to smoke. Soon, the smoker and the cigarettes are together all the time, but they keep their relationship a secret from parents and teachers. By the time others find out about it, smokers and cigarettes have developed a relationship that may last a lifetime.

A Step in the Right Direction

What was your relationship with cigarettes like when you first started smoking? Did you wonder, "What is it like to smoke? How do you do it? How do I make myself not cough? Am I doing it right?" You had to *learn* how to smoke. How long did it take until you became attached to cigarettes? Understanding this relationship will help you stay clean and free.

A Suggestion

Compare your relationship with cigarettes with another relationship you began about the same time. What similarities do you see?

Are You Experiencing Withdrawal Symptoms?

Quitting smoking is hard to do. In the early days after quitting smoking, recovering smokers are often overwhelmed with frustration. They feel irritable and have mood swings. Their friends lose patience with them and avoid them. They can't sleep, can't stay awake, can't concentrate, and can't get enough to eat. Many people decide they cannot tolerate the discomfort of withdrawal and return to smoking, saying, "I'm not going to *suffer* like this." Sometimes, their families encourage them to go back to smoking, saying, "You've *suffered* enough" or "We've put up with enough of your *suffering*."

A Step in the Right Direction

Have you been suffering with symptoms like these? The *I Ching*, a book of Buddhist philosophy, says, "Suffering is optional." Yes, you have had some withdrawal symptoms (as do most smokers when they quit), but why should you "suffer"? Pain is a physical fact; suffering is how you experience it. Will you allow the symptoms of nicotine withdrawal to distract you from your goal?

A Suggestion

If you are not ready to give up suffering just yet, try using this strategy to regain control. Allow yourself an hour a day to really suffer; use this time to complain, yell, curse, moan, and question your decision to quit smoking. Then use the other twenty-three hours productively.

Euphoric Recall

Many recovering smokers can easily recall the pleasure they got from smoking but do not remember the pain. This is called "euphoric recall." They remember how good a cigarette tasted, how the first rush of nicotine felt each morning, and how satisfying it was to smoke a cigarette. They forget that their smoking also caused coughs, fatigue, bronchitis, and shortness of breath. Even recovering smokers with cancer and heart disease admit that they always enjoyed smoking, and some of them fully intend to smoke again.

A Step in the Right Direction

When you think back to your years of smoking, do you secretly smile, remembering how much you enjoyed smoking? You have come this far in recovery because you have focused on the *consequences* of smoking instead of its pleasures. This strategy has worked so far, but it will not be enough to keep you clean and free indefinitely.

A Suggestion

Set out on the next stage of your journey of recovery. If you catch yourself thinking pleasant thoughts about smoking, remind yourself of the reasons that you quit smoking, and then reframe each reason in terms of being a nonsmoker. For instance, "I quit smoking to stay healthy. . . . As a healthy nonsmoker, I'll be able to reach my goals in life."

Six Aspects of Nicotine and Tobacco Dependence

There are six important aspects of nicotine and tobacco dependence: the physical dependence on the drug nicotine, the use of nicotine to alter moods and feelings, the enjoyment of inhaling and blowing smoke, the image created by the tobacco companies for their products, the associations smokers develop with smoking, and the rituals smokers create around their smoking. To quit smoking, smokers must successfully deal with each of these six aspects of nicotine and tobacco dependence.

A Step in the Right Direction

How much of your smoking was due to each of these aspects of nicotine and tobacco dependence?

1. To the chemical stimulation provided by the nicotine in cigarettes?
2. To the ability of the drug nicotine to alter your moods and feelings?
3. To the smoke, the fire, and the actions of smoking?
4. To the image of being a smoker, or being the smoker of a certain brand?
5. To the things associated with smoking (such as drinking coffee or eating a meal)?
6. To the rituals of smoking (such as the way you handled a cigarette)?

Which aspect of smoking was the hardest for you to give up?

Nicotine Is a Drug

There are six important aspects to nicotine and tobacco dependence: the physical dependence on the drug nicotine, the use of nicotine to alter moods and feelings, the enjoyment of inhaling and blowing smoke, the image created by the tobacco companies for their products, the associations smokers develop with smoking, and the rituals smokers create around their smoking. Today, we will look at how the drug *nicotine* is responsible for part of the dependence on smoking.

Nicotine is a powerful, addicting drug with stimulant properties similar to those of cocaine and amphetamines. Medical research has shown that nicotine causes a stronger physical dependence than heroin, cocaine, alcohol, caffeine, or marijuana.

A Step in the Right Direction

Did you smoke to give yourself a chemical lift? If cigarettes did not contain nicotine, would you have smoked as long as you did? If you smoked primarily because of the stimulation from nicotine, you are in danger of relapsing when you get tired or sleepy, or when you stay up later than usual. What can you do to avoid relapsing in these situations?

A Suggestion

Set an earlier bedtime for yourself for the first three months of your recovery, and make a commitment to getting enough sleep every night.

Nicotine Alters Moods and Feelings

There are six important aspects to nicotine and tobacco dependence: the physical dependence on the drug nicotine, the use of nicotine to alter moods and feelings, the enjoyment of inhaling and blowing smoke, the image created by the tobacco companies for their products, the associations smokers develop with smoking, and the rituals smokers create around their smoking. Today, we will look at how nicotine *alters moods and feelings.*

Smokers turn to cigarettes to deal with anger, hurt, embarrassment, guilt, and frustration. Nicotine cannot solve any of the problems that cause these emotions, but it does cover up the feelings temporarily. After smokers quit, they have to deal with all these emotions directly, and many do not know how to do that.

A Step in the Right Direction

Which strong feelings have you had to deal with as a nonsmoker that you avoided as a smoker? Can you recall times when you used cigarettes to deal with these feelings? What are you doing to deal with the emotional turmoil in your life since you quit smoking?

A Suggestion

Identify a time in the last week when you experienced each of the five emotions listed above: anger, hurt, embarrassment, guilt, and frustration. How did you deal with these feelings without smoking?

Fire and Smoke Attract People to Cigarettes

There are six important aspects to nicotine and tobacco dependence: the physical dependence on the drug nicotine, the use of nicotine to alter moods and feelings, the enjoyment of inhaling and blowing smoke, the image created by the tobacco companies for their products, the associations smokers develop with smoking, and the rituals smokers create around their smoking. Today, we will look at how the *fire and smoke* attract people to smoking.

There is something very special about fire and smoke. Campers gather around a campfire to share songs, stories, and fellowship; families come together to sit in front of the fireplace on cold winter evenings; smokers huddle together, sharing the warmth of their cigarettes. A cigarette without smoke would be nothing but a nicotine stick.

A Step in the Right Direction

When you were smoking, what were some of the things you did with your cigarette smoke? Did you teach yourself some special tricks, like blowing smoke rings or blowing the smoke out your nose? You have quit smoking, but do you still miss the smoke? If you do, this could be a relapse issue for you.

A Suggestion

When you catch yourself reminiscing about smoking, stop this line of thinking by reminding yourself that the smoke contains the carcinogens and carbon monoxide that you want to avoid.

Advertising Creates an Image for Cigarette Brands

There are six important aspects to nicotine and tobacco dependence: the physical dependence on the drug nicotine, the use of nicotine to alter moods and feelings, the enjoyment of inhaling and blowing smoke, the image created by the tobacco companies for their products, the associations smokers develop with smoking, and the rituals smokers create around their smoking. Today, we will look at the importance of the *images* the tobacco companies create.

Tobacco companies promote a particular image of their customers through advertising. Certain brands are marketed to appeal to people who see themselves as bold and adventurous, sophisticated and refined, fun loving and spirited, independent and self-assured, outgoing and athletic, or macho and carefree. The tobacco in all cigarettes is essentially the same, so cigarettes are advertised in different ways to create a unique image for each brand.

A Step in the Right Direction

Did you start smoking because of the image smokers projected? What is the image of a smoker of the brand you most recently smoked?

A Suggestion

Collect several cigarette ads that catch your eye. What image are they promoting? How might these images of smokers and smoking attract *you* back to smoking?

Associations with Smoking Make Quitting Difficult

There are six important aspects to nicotine and tobacco dependence: the physical dependence on the drug nicotine, the use of nicotine to alter moods and feelings, the enjoyment of inhaling and blowing smoke, the image created by the tobacco companies for their products, the associations smokers develop with smoking, and the rituals smokers create around their smoking. Today, we will look at the many things smokers *associate* with smoking.

After smoking for twenty or thirty years, smokers associate a cigarette with just about everything they do, for example: drinking coffee, eating a meal, talking on the telephone, driving a car, getting off work, having sex, and seeing another person smoking a cigarette.

A Step in the Right Direction

What people, places, things, and situations did you associate with smoking? What happens when you are with those people or in those situations now? What can you do to avoid relapsing in those situations?

A Suggestion

Place a little red sticker on every object you associate with smoking—on the dashboard of your car, on your coffee cup at work, and on the handset of the telephone. Then whenever you see a sticker, momentarily stop and remind yourself why you have quit smoking.

Create Some New Rituals

There are six important aspects to nicotine and tobacco dependence: the physical dependence on the drug nicotine, the use of nicotine to alter moods and feelings, the enjoyment of inhaling and blowing smoke, the image created by the tobacco companies for their products, the associations smokers develop with smoking, and the rituals smokers create around their smoking. Today, we will look at *rituals*.

Smokers develop rituals around their smoking: where they carry their cigarettes; how they open a new pack; how they take a cigarette out; how they light one, hold one, puff on one, and put one out. These rituals help smokers feel more in control. Smoking rituals are as much a part of nicotine and tobacco dependence as the nicotine and the tobacco.

A Step in the Right Direction

How did your smoking rituals help you deal with stress? For some smokers, their rituals are *more* important than the nicotine in their cigarettes. Continuing your old rituals may put you at risk for relapse.

A Suggestion

Create some new rituals to replace the ones associated with smoking. Arrange your desk in a new way, go to work using a different route, or think of a new dinnertime ritual. Your new rituals will help keep you from thinking about smoking.

What Did You Like about Smoking?

Most smokers enjoy smoking; some enjoy it more than just about anything else. They give many different reasons for enjoying smoking, such as to relax, to be sociable, to feel in control, and to deal with stress, boredom, anger, loneliness, and frustration. Smokers put a high value on their smoking. As long as they value being a smoker more highly than being a nonsmoker, they will not be able to quit. If recovering smokers do not put an ever greater value on being a nonsmoker, they will eventually return to smoking.

A Step in the Right Direction

What did you like about smoking? Now that you are no longer smoking, your challenge is to stay clean and free.

A Suggestion

Evaluate your danger of relapse today. In your journal, list the eight reasons mentioned above of why smokers use cigarettes (to relax, to be sociable, to feel in control, and to deal with stress, boredom, anger, loneliness, and frustration). Think about each individual reason, and indicate whether you used cigarettes for that purpose. Then describe how you are dealing with each issue now that you no longer smoke. You've been successful so far, so you're doing something right. Use this exercise to identify some of the strategies that have been working for you.

Getting Personal

One of the most common reasons smokers give for deciding to quit smoking is that they just finally decided to quit. This is a sensible reason, but it may not be *personal* enough for them to recover. When smokers give this reason for quitting, there is usually a secret reason behind it that they are reluctant to reveal.

A Step in the Right Direction

In order to recover—not just quit smoking—you must make your reasons more personal.

A Suggestion

Respond to the following questions in your journal.

- Did you feel foolish or embarrassed because you were still smoking when most of your friends had already quit?
- Did you ever pretend you were a nonsmoker when you were with a group of nonsmokers?
- Did you ever ask to sit in the nonsmoking section of a restaurant because you didn't want to admit you still smoked?
- Do you have secret reasons for quitting that you haven't shared with anyone? At the very least, will you confide in your journal?

These First Weeks Are Critical

Recovering smokers are most vulnerable to relapse in the first week after quitting. At that point, their nicotine level has dropped to zero and they are beginning to feel the symptoms of withdrawal. These symptoms—irritability, difficulty concentrating, mood swings, insomnia, and craving for a cigarette—build in intensity. Research shows that 25 percent of people who have quit smoking relapse within the first two days; an additional 25 percent relapse during the next week. By the end of the first year, 88 percent have relapsed. Each year thereafter, a certain percent return to smoking—even twenty years after quitting.

A Step in the Right Direction

Did you think about smoking again in the first two days after you quit smoking? In the first week? Now that you have not smoked for several weeks, you have made it past the most critical period. That's the good news. The bad news is that you are still at risk for relapse—and always will be. Therefore, you must do something positive every day to stay clean and free.

A Suggestion

Take action today to prevent a relapse. When did you have the time and the opportunity today to do work on your recovery, but chose to do something else? Are you willing to make a commitment to yourself and to your future to take *every* opportunity to make progress during this next week?

Old Friends Can Be Relapse Triggers

Wanting to be a part of your old crowd again can be a trigger to relapse. Smokers tend to hang around with other smokers, particularly since there are fewer and fewer places where smoking is permitted nowadays. After quitting smoking, recovering smokers often feel lost—they don't yet consider themselves nonsmokers, but they know they don't belong with the smokers anymore.

A Step in the Right Direction

Your recovery is a serious threat to the self-esteem of your friends who still smoke. They may try to make you feel guilty about quitting with comments like this: "You're just not the same since you quit smoking. . . . I miss the old you. It seems like you don't have time for me anymore." That could really hurt. If you feel guilty or lonely in a situation like this, you might be tempted to smoke again. What can you do instead?

A Suggestion

Tell your friend, "I miss smoking with you, and I still want to be your friend. But if I start smoking again, I'll miss being a nonsmoker even more."

Your Body Is Healing

Most people know that smoking causes lung cancer. But many people are unaware that it also increases the risk of other cancers, including cancer of the breast, bladder, pancreas, colon, cervix, stomach, larynx, and mouth. Smoking also causes emphysema, bronchitis, coronary heart disease, stroke, arteriosclerosis, and damage to the immune system. It increases the risk of developing cataracts, ulcers, and sinus infections. It also causes facial wrinkles and bad breath. Many smokers say, "Sure, smoking causes problems, *but it won't happen to me.*" Sometimes they shrug and say, "Well, ya gotta die from something." When smokers make statements like these, they are trying to avoid dealing with the truth.

A Step in the Right Direction

Do you know someone who has suffered physical illness due to smoking? Have you suffered physical illness due to smoking? How many of your sick days over the last five years were due to smoking? On average, smokers get at least one lost-time illness each year more than nonsmokers. Now that you are no longer smoking, your body has started to heal, and it will continue to heal for the next ten years.

A Suggestion

Review your health record over the last few years. What improvements are you hoping for? By staying clean and free, how will you be a healthier person in the years to come?

Dealing with Relapse Triggers

Relapse triggers are everywhere. In order to stay clean and free, recovering smokers must identify them and make plans for dealing with them.

A Step in the Right Direction

You will encounter many relapse triggers during your first year of recovery. Such everyday situations as shaving or putting on makeup, getting stuck in traffic, and drinking a cup of coffee can remind you of smoking. What can you do about them?

A Suggestion

Make a list of everyday situations you associate with smoking. Each day this week, choose one and think of something to do in that situation that will prevent you from smoking. Write the details of your plans in your journal. For example:

- Instead of smoking while shaving or putting on makeup, you could sing. It doesn't matter how well you sing—what matters is doing whatever it takes to avoid a relapse.
- While stuck in traffic, you could turn on the radio and drum along with the music, using your steering wheel as a drum set.
- You could switch from coffee to a beverage you don't associate with smoking for a while, such as hot water with lemon.

Be creative! The more personal your alternatives are, the better they will work.

Most Children Recognize Joe Camel

People develop many attitudes early in life. A recent study showed that 31 percent of three-year-olds and 91 percent of six-year-olds recognize the Joe Camel cartoon character to mean *smoking Camel cigarettes.* These children are used to seeing cartoon characters; they look forward to seeing Joe Camel ads the same way they look forward to seeing other cartoons. Psychologists predict that when these children get older, their positive attitude about Joe Camel will make them highly likely to become smokers. The R. J. Reynolds Company would like them to become Camel smokers. In 1987, before the Joe Camel promotion began, 0.5 percent of smokers under the age of nineteen chose Camel as their favorite brand; in 1991, 32.8 percent of smokers under the age of nineteen preferred Camel. R. J. Reynolds insists that they do not advertise to children, but the Joe Camel promotions have only produced a substantial effect on the smoking behavior of children, not on the smoking behavior of adults.

A Step in the Right Direction

Did your attitudes about smoking begin in childhood?

A Suggestion

Describe how smoking was a part of your passage from childhood to adulthood. Did you look forward to the day you would be able to smoke? What influenced you to select your first brand? How did you feel when you learned to smoke with confidence?

Depression Can Be Treated

Some days just don't go well; on such days, people often use the word "depressed" to describe how they feel. But when psychologists and psychiatrists use the term "major depression," they are referring to an imbalance in the brain chemicals that control mood. About 10 percent of Americans who never smoked become clinically depressed at some time during their lives, but major depression strikes about 30 percent of Americans who have been daily smokers. Also, people with depression smoke more and have a harder time quitting than people who are not depressed. Many people with depression appear to be self-medicating their depression with nicotine.

A Step in the Right Direction

Medical doctors have many effective treatments for depression today; there is no reason for any person with major depression to go untreated. Depression is a serious illness, leading to family problems, work problems, physical illness, and suicide.

A Suggestion

If you have had crying spells, loss of energy, thoughts of suicide, insomnia, or a change in your appetite, you may be depressed. If your symptoms persist, protect yourself and your recovery: tell your doctor or counselor how you feel and request an evaluation for depression.

Breaking through Denial

As long as their thoughts and feelings are controlled by their dependence on nicotine and tobacco, smokers cannot see how tobacco dominates their lives. This is called *denial,* the unconscious resistance to accepting a painful truth. Smokers defend their cigarettes and make excuses for their smoking, while their bodies continue to deteriorate from the toxic chemicals in cigarette smoke. A typical denial statement would be, "I'm just stepping outside for a breath of fresh air," when the real purpose is to smoke.

A Step in the Right Direction

How did you defend your cigarettes and your smoking? Do you see active smokers around you who are still in denial? How can understanding denial help you stay clean and free?

A Suggestion

Think back to when you were a smoker in denial. What might someone have said to you that would have helped you break through your denial earlier?

- What would have gotten your attention one year ago?
- What would have gotten your attention five years ago?
- What would have gotten your attention the day you smoked your first cigarette?

Make some notes in your journal about breaking through denial.

Learning to Take Control Again

Smokers devote a lot of time to their cigarettes, sometimes more time than they spend with any one person. Smokers waste an average of two hours each day with their cigarettes—buying them, smoking them, and cleaning up after them. Smokers also average one more respiratory illness each year than nonsmokers, which means more time off from work (and perhaps in the hospital). After they quit smoking, recovering smokers discover that they have more time available to them, or more time on their hands. On the average, quitting smoking frees up an entire extra month each year for a recovering smoker.

A Step in the Right Direction

When your dependence on nicotine and tobacco was in control, it determined how you spent your time and whom you spent it with. It decided when you would stop to eat or stop to talk. Now you are learning how to take control of your life again. What have you done with the extra two hours a day you now have? Have you been so busy that you didn't notice you have more time, now that you're not smoking? If you do not make a plan to use this time wisely, it can become a trigger for relapse.

A Suggestion

Make some notes in your journal about how you use your time.

Staying Clean and Free

Eliminating relapse triggers is one of the most difficult and important challenges facing a recovering smoker. To be successful, recovering smokers must eliminate as many relapse triggers as they can.

A Step in the Right Direction

The tobacco companies did not stop making cigarettes just because you quit smoking, and the world is full of relapse triggers. Which relapse triggers have you eliminated? Which ones have you been unable to do anything about?

A Suggestion

You can eliminate relapse triggers by "burning your bridges" as you go. If you used to take a coffee break (and had a cigarette) with a group of co-workers, tell your old friends you can't take breaks with them now because their smoking would be a relapse trigger for you. If the people in your carpool smoke on the way to work, get into a carpool with nonsmokers. If you go to an AA meeting where there is a lot of smoke in the room, start attending a nonsmoking meeting. Tell your old friends, "Staying clean and free is very important. I have to make a change to protect my recovery." Which bridges have you already burned? (List a few in your journal.) Which ones do you still need to burn? (Make of list of them too.)

The Perfect Pleasure?

Many well-known writers have been smokers, including Oscar Wilde. In his book *The Picture of Dorian Gray* he wrote about his relationship with cigarettes: "A cigarette is the perfect type of a perfect pleasure. It is exquisite, and it leaves one unsatisfied."

A Step in the Right Direction

What pleasures did you get from smoking? How did cigarettes satisfy you, but still leave you unsatisfied?

A Suggestion

Make a list of the pleasures you got from smoking. By understanding what you liked about smoking, you will begin to understand your addiction better, and you will be better prepared to come up with alternatives to smoking. Here are some examples:

- Smoking relaxed me when I was tense.
- Smoking perked me up when I was drowsy.
- Smoking helped me concentrate when I needed to think clearly.
- Smoking helped me feel self-confident and in control.
- Smoking made me feel more mature when I was young.
- Smoking made me feel accepted.

Identify at least ten ways that smoking satisfied you or made you feel good.

Support from Others Can Make the Difference

Smokers often reject support from others when they set out to quit smoking. Their families and friends want to help, but their concern sometimes comes across like nagging. When their help is rejected, they often become frustrated and stop trying to help. Research shows that the support of family and friends makes staying clean and free much easier.

A Step in the Right Direction

How have you responded to the advice of family and friends? Was their encouragement helpful or did it feel like nagging? Have they been supportive since you quit smoking, or did it feel as if they were checking up on you? The next time your family or friends ask how your smoking cessation program is going, how will you respond?

A Suggestion

Use this three-part response.

- Start by saying, "Thank you for asking."
- Then tell them exactly how you have been doing.
- End by making a statement of commitment to your recovery.

For example: "Thank you for asking. It's been tough; I think about smoking every day. But I'm staying focused, and I'm not going to smoke." Or, "Thank you for asking. I've been amazed at how well I've been doing lately. I'm confident that I'm going to make it."

Do You Still Want to Smoke?

Recovering smokers frequently experience a desire to smoke again. There are three main causes for this:

- *Nicotine withdrawal symptoms.* Nearly all smokers experience withdrawal symptoms when they first quit smoking. Irritability, mood swings, difficulty concentrating, insomnia, anxiety, and an intense craving for a cigarette are typical symptoms. These symptoms may last for two or three weeks after quitting smoking.
- *Situations.* A sudden overwhelming desire for a cigarette can be created by seeing or smelling a cigarette, or being in a situation previously associated with smoking.
- *Emotions.* Experiencing strong emotions (such as embarrassment, fear, anger, or frustration) can trigger the desire to smoke because the smoker previously used cigarettes to cope with these feelings.

A Step in the Right Direction

Do you still have nicotine withdrawal symptoms? Do you still want a cigarette at certain times or in certain situations? Do strong emotions make you want a cigarette?

A Suggestion

Identify three moments from the previous day when you really wanted a cigarette. What triggered your desire to smoke?

Personal Reasons to Quit

One of the most common reasons smokers give for deciding to quit smoking is that they have damaged some furniture, clothing, or carpeting with a burning cigarette. This reason is *serious* enough for them to quit, but it may not be *personal* enough for them to recover.

A Step in the Right Direction

Your carpet can be replaced, but *you* cannot be replaced. In order to recover—not just quit smoking—you must make your reasons more personal.

A Suggestion

Respond to the following questions in your journal.

- Have you ever damaged some property with a cigarette, match, or lighter?
- Did damaging the property make you think about quitting smoking?
- Did the damage you caused also damage a friendship or a relationship? Was the relationship a lot more important than the property?
- Were you embarrassed about the damage your smoking caused? What did you say and do? Did you try to hide the damage (or think about trying to hide it)?
- If a smoker damages some of your property one day, what will you do?
- Why would anyone quit smoking for a piece of property when they won't quit smoking for their own health or to maintain a relationship?

Use Guided Imagery to Heal Your Body

Use guided imagery to improve the condition of your blood vessels.

A Step in the Right Direction

Guided imagery is a valuable strategy for relaxing your body while focusing the power of your mind. Here is a guided imagery exercise you can use; you will find others as you move through this book.

Plan to do this exercise for about five minutes. Sit in a comfortable chair or lie down, legs and arms uncrossed. Close your eyes, and breathe slowly and deeply. With each deep breath, imagine yourself becoming more and more relaxed. Focus on your breathing. Continue to breathe deeply, allowing all the concerns of the day to leave your mind as the air leaves your lungs. When your body is thoroughly relaxed, turn your attention to your arteries. Search through your arteries, the vessels that carry oxygenated blood to your heart, your brain, and the rest of your body. Cigarette smoke has scorched the lining of these arteries, and the toxic chemicals in cigarette smoke have built up thick deposits of fatty material in them. Focus the power of your mind on healing the damaged walls of your arteries. Continue to breathe deeply and relax. After about five minutes, open your eyes and notice how you feel.

A Suggestion

Use guided imagery every day to help your body and your mind heal.

What Happened to Wayne McLaren?

Wayne McLaren was one of the first cowboys who posed as the Marlboro Man for the Philip Morris Company. He was a real rodeo cowboy before he became an actor and then the Marlboro Man. In 1990, after thirty years of smoking cigarettes, he was diagnosed with lung cancer—the kind caused by smoking. After that, he became a vigorous opponent of cigarette advertising. He went to the annual shareholder's meeting of the Philip Morris Company and stood up and told his story. He suggested that the Philip Morris Company should stop selling cigarettes because they give people lung cancer. Not surprisingly, they hustled him out of the meeting and didn't give him another opportunity to talk. However, he continued to tell his story to anyone who would listen, until his lung cancer killed him in 1992 at the age of fifty-one.

A Step in the Right Direction

If you could go to the annual meeting of the shareholders of the Philip Morris Company, what would you tell them?

A Suggestion

Write a letter to the chairperson of the board of the tobacco company who made the cigarettes you used to smoke. Imagine what might happen if the company received hundreds of letters every day from recovering smokers.

Accept Support

Quitting smoking may be the hardest thing any smoker ever does. Many smokers rely on a *single* source of support when they try to quit; this puts them at risk for relapse if that source of support is not enough. Smokers improve their chances of success by seeking help and support from many sources. Doctors and counselors are one source of support; supportive family and friends are another. Here are some others:

- American Cancer Society, The FreshStart program (404-320-3333)
- American Lung Association, Freedom from Smoking program (212-315-8700)
- Seventh-Day Adventists, Breathe Free Plan (301-790-9735)
- QuitSmart (quit smoking program) (919-684-2887)
- Nicotine Anonymous (Twelve Step program) (415-750-0328)
- Hazelden Publishing and Education (helpful books, pamphlets, and tapes) (800-328-9000)

A Step in the Right Direction

Are you using a variety of sources of support to improve your chances of success?

A Suggestion

Call one of the organizations listed above to get more information and support to help you stay clean and free.

What's Most Important?

Many smokers use cigarettes to calm down after an argument. In fact, many recovering smokers want to smoke a cigarette when in conflict with another person even years after they quit smoking. Conflict makes them tense and uneasy. Some worry about losing the argument, some worry about losing the relationship, and some worry about losing both.

A Step in the Right Direction

If you are a person who tries to avoid conflict, you may feel like smoking again whenever you disagree with someone. Even after the problem is resolved, you may feel uncomfortable and unsettled, and the nagging desire for a cigarette may not go away.

A Suggestion

When you get into a conflict with someone, use the skills you have been learning to understand your needs, the needs of the other person, and the reasons for the conflict. Use the stress-reduction skills you have learned and reach out to your supporters; tell them how you feel and describe how your desire to smoke increases when you get into a conflict with someone. Most important, be sure to resolve conflicts as quickly as possible, because leaving them unresolved increases your risk of relapse. Ask yourself what is more important: proving you are right or staying clean and free? When you start looking at conflicts in this way, a lot of them seem petty.

How about Just One?

Some recovering smokers accept that they are dependent on nicotine and tobacco, but still secretly believe that smoking again would be all right in certain situations—such as serious illness, severe stress, or old age. These people are at risk for relapse *right now* because they have not fully accepted their dependence on nicotine and tobacco.

A Step in the Right Direction

Could you justify smoking again in a certain situation or if some catastrophe occurred? If your doctor told you that you had cancer and only had six months to live, would you go back to smoking? What if you had a stroke and couldn't get out of bed—would you go back to smoking? If you think you would, you will eventually be able to justify smoking again in less serious situations. In time, you would be able to justify smoking at any time, and relapse would become inevitable.

A Suggestion

If tobacco still has a grip on you, writing a "Good-bye" letter to tobacco will help you break tobacco's grip. If you have already started one, pull it out, read it over, and add things that you have learned over the last month. If you have not started one, start today. Start with "Good-bye Tobacco," and tell tobacco why you are leaving it behind.

Your Medications May Need Adjustment

The body metabolizes (processes) nicotine to cotinine and other chemicals, primarily in the liver. After a smoker quits smoking, the liver is free to process other chemicals. If that person also uses sedatives (sleeping medication or tranquilizers), antidepressants or neuroleptics (for control of a major mental illness), the rate at which these medications are broken down can increase, and the blood levels of these medications may drop. This may require an adjustment in the dosages of the medications. After a time, the liver accommodates itself to not having nicotine around and the medication levels stabilize. If the recovering smoker relapses, however, the liver will suddenly have more to do; the metabolism of the medications slows down, and their blood levels may rise. This can lead to serious complications from having too much of the medications in the bloodstream.

A Step in the Right Direction

Tell your doctor that you have quit smoking and discuss your medical treatment if you are taking any of these medications: AZT, Coumadin, DiaBeta, Depakote, desipramine, Dilantin, Elavil, Glucotrol, Klonopin, Lanoxin, nortriptyline, Paxil, phenobarbital, Prozac, Tegretol, trazadone, or Zoloft. Your doctor may want to check the blood level of your medication (if a test is available for the medication you are on) and consider adjusting your dosage.

Nicotine Replacement Is for Short-Term Use

The nicotine patch and the nicotine gum are intended for temporary use to decrease the discomfort of nicotine withdrawal. Neither the patch nor the gum is intended for long-term use. Research shows that using these products improves a smoker's chances of quitting, but that there is no value in using them longer than eight weeks. Recovering smokers who continue to use nicotine replacement products longer than three months may actually increase their chances of returning to smoking because they are still active users of the drug nicotine.

A Step in the Right Direction

Have you used nicotine replacement medication too long? Whether you used nicotine replacement medication or not, have you thought about keeping some nicotine gum or some nicotine patches around, just in case you might be tempted to smoke? Have you thought that using the patch or an occasional piece of nicotine gum would be a lot better than breaking down and having a cigarette? Using the gum or the patch in this way could put you at risk for relapse. If you give your addiction an opportunity, it will take control of your thoughts, feelings, and actions. Its appetite will not be satisfied with the gum or the patch—it will demand cigarettes.

A Suggestion

Make a commitment to yourself to not use the nicotine gum or patch longer than eight weeks.

Your Dentist Can Help You Succeed

Dentists are often the first to notice physical damage from smoking (such as injured tissues in the mouth, weakened gums, and a persistent cough). Many dentists have become actively involved in helping their patients quit smoking because they see so many dental problems in smokers. Dentists can prescribe the nicotine gum and the nicotine patch; they can provide counseling and advice; and they can refer their patients to other treatment professionals. A complete dental evaluation now includes an evaluation of any damage done by smoking to tissues in the mouth and professional advice regarding smoking.

A Step in the Right Direction

When you were still smoking, did your dentist ever comment on the effects of smoking on your teeth and gums? Did your dentist advise you to quit smoking and offer advice and assistance?

A Suggestion

If you have not seen your dentist recently, treat yourself to a professional dental cleaning. You and your dentist will undoubtedly notice how much better your breath smells. Within a few months after quitting smoking, your gums will have begun to heal. Tell your dentist about your success in quitting smoking. What do you expect he or she will say?

Learn about Your Craving Triggers

Cravings for a cigarette continue for months after quitting—sometimes for years. In order to prevent a relapse when cravings occur, recovering smokers need to identify the things that trigger their cravings. Here are some common craving triggers:

- Withdrawal symptoms: irritability, difficulty concentrating, mood swings
- Depressed mood or anxiety that persists beyond the first month after quitting
- People, places, and situations that trigger strong emotions
- Painful memories from the past that were never resolved
- Conflicts with other people

A Step in the Right Direction

Which of these five kinds of craving triggers have been a problem for you? Was one of them a problem today? How can you reduce the effect of these craving triggers on you so that you can stay clean and free?

A Suggestion

In your journal, write out a detailed schedule of your plans for tomorrow. Where do you expect these craving triggers to be strongest? What plans can you make to deal with them *before* they occur? List your planned strategies on your schedule along with your other plans—using them successfully is probably more important than most of your appointments.

Toss Out Your Old Cigarettes

Recovering smokers frequently find half-empty packs of cigarettes in various places for months or years after they quit smoking. Finding these old cigarettes can be a relapse trigger. The smell of the tobacco (however stale) and the feel of the cigarette bring back memories of smoking.

A Step in the Right Direction

Have you already come across forgotten packs of cigarettes in a drawer, in a coat pocket, or on a dusty shelf? What did you do? Did you consider smoking one—even for an instant? Did you immediately toss the cigarettes away, or like some people, did you carefully put them back where you found them? If you kept the cigarettes, you are dangerously close to relapsing. What is your plan for dealing with old cigarettes the next time you find some?

A Suggestion

Get rid of these relapse triggers immediately. Experience has shown that tossing cigarettes out quickly and without ceremony is the best way. Some recovering smokers decide to make a major ritual out of throwing away cigarettes, like destroying them one by one or burying them in the backyard. Doing that will only remind you about smoking even more. Instead, flush the cigarettes down the commode as soon as you find them. Eliminating reminders about smoking will help you stay clean and free.

When the Addiction Is in Control

In the past, psychiatric patients at state mental hospitals were rewarded with cigarettes. If the patients made their beds, they got a cigarette. If they brushed their teeth, they got a cigarette. If they argued with the staff, no cigarettes. The staff of these hospitals knew that cigarettes were more rewarding to these patients than anything else, so they purposely kept the patients addicted in order to control their behavior. These patients were so heavily dependent on nicotine and tobacco that they would comply with any request to receive a cigarette. Although most doctors encourage their patients to stop smoking, most psychiatrists still do not address this issue with their patients, and some state mental hospitals continue to use cigarettes to control their patients' behavior.

A Step in the Right Direction

How did cigarettes control your behavior?

A Suggestion

Recall how you rewarded yourself with a cigarette when you were still smoking. These situations are similar to the way state mental hospitals controlled their patients. Did you smoke a cigarette after completing an assignment or a meeting? (Finish the job—then you can have a cigarette.) Did you smoke as soon as you left work? (Work all day—then you can have a cigarette.) Did you smoke after meals? (Finish your dinner—then you can have a cigarette.)

Food and Beverage Relapse Triggers

Smokers build up many associations between things they eat or drink and smoking. Some examples include coffee, desserts, Mexican food, barbecue, beer, and margaritas.

A Step in the Right Direction

When you were still smoking, which foods did you associate with smoking? Since you quit smoking, have there been times when you ate something and suddenly wanted a cigarette? After years of having coffee with a cigarette, you undoubtedly associate the two tastes with each other. Even though it has been some time since you smoked a cigarette, you may still be reminded of smoking every time you drink a cup of coffee. Alcoholic drinks, especially beer and margaritas, are relapse triggers for some recovering smokers. Do you associate these or other tastes with smoking? What have you done to reduce your desire to smoke when something you ate or drank reminded you of smoking?

A Suggestion

Identify the specific foods and beverages that still make you want to smoke. List them in your journal in order of how strong a relapse trigger they are for you. In order to remain clean and free, are you willing to give these things up until your recovery is stronger?

Environmental Tobacco Smoke

Environmental tobacco smoke (ETS) refers to three kinds of involuntary smoking:

- Sidestream smoke (smoke in the air that comes from the burning end of a cigarette)
- Secondhand smoke (smoke inhaled and then exhaled into the air by a smoker)
- Transplacental smoke (smoke inhaled by a pregnant woman, absorbed into her body, and then passed to her unborn child through the placenta)

Components of ETS include particulate matter (bits of soot), carbon monoxide, chemicals that cause cancer (nitrosamines, pyrethrins, benzene, radon), chemicals that cause arteriosclerosis, vaporized heavy metals (arsenic, lead, radioactive polonium-210, cadmium), and chemicals that irritate the lungs.

A Step in the Right Direction

When you were a smoker, did you contribute to environmental tobacco smoke? What do you do now when someone else does?

A Suggestion

Before you confront a person who is contaminating the air you breathe with tobacco smoke, practice how you will do it. Choose a situation you are likely to encounter, such as seeing a person smoking in the nonsmoking section of a restaurant or riding in a cab with a cab driver who is smoking. Make some notes in your journal about what you will say and do in this situation.

Support Your Doctor

Doctors usually avoid talking to their patients about quitting smoking. In 1950, part of the reason was that half of all doctors smoked. Today only a handful of doctors smoke, so there must be another reason. Many doctors say they just don't have the time to talk to their patients about smoking. Some realize that they received very little education about nicotine dependence during their training and they feel inadequate to advise their patients. Others say they never learned how to counsel patients. Still others say they don't want to embarrass people by talking about private behaviors. Finally, many doctors say they don't deal with smoking because very few of their patients actually quit, and this low success rate has discouraged them from dealing with the issue.

A Step in the Right Direction

How many of the doctors you have seen in your life advised you to quit smoking? Was your decision to quit smoking influenced by a doctor? What can you do to improve this situation?

A Suggestion

Write a note to your doctor, telling him or her that you have quit smoking; if he or she had once suggested that you quit smoking, mention in your note that a doctor's advice can help a smoker quit. Your success in quitting smoking will teach your doctor that helping smokers quit is worth the time and effort.

Honesty in Advertising

The tobacco companies stopped advertising on television in the 1960s and shifted much of their advertising to magazines. Cigarette ads quickly became a major source of revenue for many magazines, including *Sports Illustrated, Ebony, Newsweek, Time, People, Rolling Stone,* and *Jet.* Today, most magazines accept tobacco advertising, although an increasing number do not. The tobacco companies say their ads are intended to help them keep their customers and to draw other smokers to their brand. However, these ads also attract people who have never smoked to smoking, and they entice recovering smokers to start again.

A Step in the Right Direction

The tobacco companies lose two to three thousand good customers every day—some quit; many die. The tobacco companies want to replace their lost customers with new ones; their ads are designed to bring in new customers. As a recovering smoker, you are also vulnerable to these ads, but you do not have to give in to them.

A Suggestion

Pick an ad for cigarettes that catches your attention. Study it carefully. How does the ad *lie?* Why do so many people believe these lies? Why did you believe them for so long?

Reach Out to Stay Clean and Free

Automatic behaviors keep smokers hooked. A typical automatic behavior is reaching for a cigarette when the telephone rings. For some people, phone calls always mean trouble: bad news, extra work, or conflict. These people associate the sound of the telephone ringing with stress, and they use cigarettes to deal with stress. Over time, they come to associate the ringing of the telephone with smoking a cigarette. Once the automatic behavior becomes established, they reach for a cigarette regardless of what the phone call is about.

A Step in the Right Direction

When you were still smoking, did you smoke while talking on the telephone? What kinds of phone calls really made you want to smoke? Years after their last cigarette, many recovering smokers continue to think about smoking when they hear a phone ring. What can you do to break the association between the ringing of the telephone and smoking a cigarette?

A Suggestion

Keep a pad of paper and a pen next to every phone in your house and by your phone at work. Each time the phone rings, write "Clean and free" on a piece of paper before you answer the phone. Eventually, this reminder of your progress in recovery will replace the association between the ringing of the telephone and smoking.

Smoking Fantasies Can Be Relapse Triggers

At some point in their recovery, many recovering smokers start fantasizing about smoking again. These fantasies often lead to relapse.

A Step in the Right Direction

Relapses begin when smoking becomes possible, which may be a long time before you actually light a cigarette. Smoking becomes *possible* when you start thinking how nice it would be to smoke again. You must halt these fantasies as soon as they start, because they build on each other. If you imagine yourself smoking after a meal, it will be easier to imagine yourself smoking with a cup of coffee in the morning. Then you might imagine yourself smoking in the car, after sex, or before going to bed. These fantasies are extremely dangerous because they don't include the consequences of smoking. Fantasies about smoking often precede a relapse. Have you fantasized about smoking?

A Suggestion

The next time you imagine yourself enjoying a cigarette, also imagine yourself coughing and choking on thick, searing smoke; imagine filling up your lungs with black, deadly smoke. Replacing one fantasy with another can help you stay clean and free.

Attitudes Develop in Childhood

Attitudes change very slowly. Attitudes learned in adulthood can be changed with information and positive action, but attitudes learned in childhood are so deeply ingrained that they may never change. Cigarette smoke is an example. Children see adults and other children smoking and wonder what smoking is like. They are fascinated by the fire and the smoke; they see smokers exhale through their noses and blow smoke rings. *They* aren't allowed to play with matches and lighters—but smokers are. These observations lead children to develop a positive attitude about smoking. Those who start smoking discover it is very hard to quit smoking later.

A Step in the Right Direction

What were your attitudes about cigarette smoke before you started smoking? Do you recall watching someone smoking and wondering what it was like? Did you enjoy the smell of cigarette smoke? These positive attitudes about smoking have made it hard for you to quit smoking—hard, but not impossible.

A Suggestion

Describe in your journal how you were attracted to smoking because of the fire and smoke. When did your attitudes about cigarette smoke begin to change? Now that you have quit smoking, what are your attitudes about cigarette smoke?

Smokers Threaten Your Recovery

Living with a smoker is a serious threat to the recovery of a person who has recently quit smoking. Research shows that relapse rates more than double when a recovering smoker lives with a person who still smokes. Relapse rates are very high even when the smoker only smokes outside. Having a smoker in the house is a constant reminder of smoking. Research also shows that when smokers who live together quit at the same time, they can support each other tremendously.

A Step in the Right Direction

Is there a smoker in your house? Do visitors smoke in your house? Do you have a close friend who is a smoker? Do people you work with still smoke? The closer you are to a smoker and the more you are around smoking, the more you will be reminded of smoking; this increases your risk of relapse. What can you do to minimize this risk?

A Suggestion

Eliminate as many reminders of smoking as possible. Tell visitors that your home is smokefree. If you live or work with smokers, remind them that it is their responsibility to remove evidence of their smoking (cigarette butts, ashes, and smoking paraphernalia) from your living and working space. If they don't support your recovery, what sort of friends are they?

Protect Your Health and Your Recovery

Tobacco smoke contains over four thousand identified chemicals, including formaldehyde (embalming fluid), cyanide (used to execute convicted criminals in the gas chamber), radon (a radioactive gas), carbon monoxide (which people sometimes use to commit suicide), and benzene (which causes cancer). It also contains a number of toxic heavy metals, including arsenic, lead, cadmium, aluminum, and radioactive polonium-210. Smokers inhale these toxic chemicals with their cigarette smoke and blow some of them back out for nonsmokers to breathe. The U.S. Environmental Protection Agency lists this "passive smoke" as a serious health threat.

A Step in the Right Direction

When you were smoking, did people try to get you to put out your cigarette? If so, how did you react? When you were smoking, did you think about the toxic chemicals you released into the air for others to breathe? Now your health and your recovery may be threatened when others smoke near you. What will you say to a smoker whose cigarette is contaminating the air you breathe?

A Suggestion

Imagine several situations where someone's smoking could bother you. Write down what you could say that might convince that person to put out the cigarette. How would you have reacted to someone saying these things to you when you were still smoking?

Your Health Will Improve

Research shows that smokers' health begins to improve very soon after they stop smoking. Bronchitis improves in four days, the risk of having a heart attack drops within one year, and the risk of getting lung cancer drops in two years. After five years of being clean and free, recovering smokers' risk of having a heart attack, lung cancer, or a stroke is the same as that of people who never smoked. Stopping smoking is the best thing smokers can do to improve their health.

A Step in the Right Direction

Which health consequences of smoking have you been concerned about? Which ones have you personally suffered? Which ones have happened to a friend or relative? Most smokers know someone who has suffered a medical problem from smoking, but they usually want to believe that smoking was not the cause. Only after quitting smoking can they see the truth.

A Suggestion

Describe in your journal the improvements you have seen in your health since you quit smoking. Is your heartbeat steadier? Have you stopped coughing so much? Are you breathing easier? Do you have more endurance? Now that you are no longer smoking, what do you think children should be told about the health consequences of smoking?

A Short History of Tobacco

Over the years, tobacco has been used in a variety of ways: chewed, held in a corner of the mouth (moist snuff), sniffed up the nose (dry snuff), swallowed, and smoked. Tobacco can be smoked in the form of cigars or cigarettes, or in a pipe. Different methods of using tobacco have been popular at different points in history. The Indians of North, Central, and South America smoked tobacco in pipes (usually held in the mouth, but sometimes held in the nose). The Indians of the Northwest Coast also ground tobacco into a fine powder and sniffed it up their noses. In the eighteenth and nineteenth centuries, Europeans preferred pipes and cigars, Asians preferred fine dry snuff, and Americans preferred chewing tobacco. Cigarettes did not become popular until early in the twentieth century, after the invention of the cigarette rolling machine. Once cigarettes were easily available and relatively inexpensive, they became much more popular than all other forms of tobacco. Today, about 100 trillion cigarettes are smoked each year.

A Step in the Right Direction

Why did you choose cigarettes? If you had lived a hundred years ago, how do you think you would have used tobacco? Why do you think cigarettes became so popular?

Your Senses Can Be Relapse Triggers

The five senses often provoke a desire to smoke. Lifetime smokers will give themselves a jolt of nicotine about two million times during their lives, each one associated with sensory experiences: the sounds of the crinkle of cellophane and the snap of a lighter, the smooth feel of a cigarette, the aroma of tobacco and smoke, the flavor of tobacco smoke, and the images of the cigarette's glowing tip and the smoke curling upward.

A Step in the Right Direction

Have your senses picked up relapse triggers?

- Which sounds still remind you of smoking?
- Which sensations still remind you of smoking?
- Which smells still remind you of smoking?
- Which tastes still remind you of smoking?
- Which sights still remind you of smoking?

A Suggestion

You can deal with the relapse triggers of your senses by using your senses. Whenever you are reminded of smoking by a sound, sensation, smell, taste, or sight associated with smoking, take out your *Keep Quit!* medallion. Roll it between your fingers, tap it on the table—bite it if you have to—and say to yourself, "I can get through this without smoking."

Make Friends Who Are Clean and Free

Everyone needs to feel like a part of a group. Smokers tend to associate with other smokers and nonsmokers tend to associate with nonsmokers. When smokers quit, they often feel uncomfortable with their old friends but do not yet feel comfortable with nonsmokers. Eventually, they develop a new group of friends who are nonsmokers, but it may take some time. Until they do, they may feel adrift, without a group of people who understand them. If recovering smokers miss their old smoking friends a lot, they will have a hard time staying clean and free.

A Step in the Right Direction

Do you miss the group of friends you used to smoke with? Have you developed new friendships with nonsmokers? If you spend much time around old friends who smoke, you will be at a high risk of relapsing. How can you decrease this risk?

A Suggestion

Make a decision about your priorities. You have three basic choices:

- Spend more time with your nonsmoking friends.
- Develop new friendships with other nonsmokers.
- Encourage your old smoking friends to quit.

Which choice will be the most comfortable for you?

What Happened to R. J. Reynolds Jr.?

R. J. Reynolds Jr. was the son of the founder of the Reynolds Tobacco Company. His father, R. J. Sr., chewed plug tobacco, and he founded the company to produce plug and twist chewing tobacco in Winston, North Carolina, in 1874. Chewing tobacco was the most popular form of tobacco at the time, and R. J. Sr. did not start making cigarettes until 1913. His first cigarette was Camel, a blend of burley and flue-cured tobacco; it soon became the most popular brand in America. Later, the company began selling Winston. R. J. Reynolds Jr., who took over the company after his father's death, smoked Camels and Winstons most of his life. He died at the age of fifty-eight from emphysema. During the last few years of his life, his lungs were so bad that he could not go outside; even taking a few steps exhausted him. But he didn't stop smoking, and to the day he died, he never accepted that his smoking had anything to do with his lung disease.

A Step in the Right Direction

How did smoking damage your body? Do you still have trouble accepting that the cigarettes you loved so much did this damage to you?

A Suggestion

Read the book *The Gilded Leaf* by Patrick Reynolds and Tom Shachtman; it tells the story of the Reynolds family and shows how powerful denial can be.

Late Nights Can Be Relapse Triggers

Smoking is often associated with staying up late at night. As the evening wears on and everyone gets sleepier, smokers use the nicotine in cigarettes to help them stay alert. People also stay up late at parties and at nightclubs, where smokers gather together and smoke together. After they quit smoking, recovering smokers may still associate late hours with smoking, and they may have trouble concentrating without the chemical stimulation of nicotine. Staying up late becomes a dangerous relapse trigger for many recovering smokers.

A Step in the Right Direction

When you were still smoking, did you smoke more late at night? Did you smoke more at parties and in clubs? The next time you are up late or at a party or a nightclub, your chances of relapse will increase. How can you deal with this relapse trigger?

A Suggestion

Think of a day since you quit smoking when you stayed up later than usual. Were you doing something you associate with smoking? How close did you come to lighting up again? If late nights are a relapse trigger for you, decide today to turn down the next invitation you get to a late-night social function. The next morning, write your thoughts and feelings about missing the evening in your journal. Was it worth it to stay clean and free?

Driving Alone Can Be a Relapse Trigger

Driving a car gives people a feeling of anonymity in public that they do not get elsewhere. Most smokers smoke while driving a car; their cars become private smoking rooms. Driving alone can be a serious relapse trigger for recovering smokers who smoked a lot in their cars. Being in a car encourages relapse because it feels isolated like a private place. One key to preventing relapse in this situation is to realize that a single cigarette leads back to regular smoking. Driving alone encourages recovering smokers to smoke "just one" while driving.

A Step in the Right Direction

When you were still smoking, did you often smoke while driving alone? Since you quit smoking, have you thought about smoking while driving alone? Even if you have gotten the cigarette smell out of your car, you will still encounter many relapse triggers. When you pass billboards advertising cigarettes, what thoughts cross your mind? The last time that you stopped for gas and saw cigarettes for sale behind the counter, did you consider buying a pack? Did you ever think that you could smoke in your car and no one would know? Would *you* know?

"Free" Cigarettes Are Not Free

The tobacco companies spend around $3.5 billion each year promoting their products. They spend a lot of that money giving out free samples of tobacco products at sporting events, fairs, concerts, and even on street corners. They do this to introduce new brands and remind people about their regular brands. They hope to attract children, to get smokers to switch brands, and to entice recovering smokers to start again.

A Step in the Right Direction

Do you have a hard time turning down something that's free? "Free samples" of cigarettes are anything but free—they could cost you your life. Tobacco companies are hoping you will accept their samples, smoke a few, and then go back to regular daily smoking. How will you react when offered free cigarettes?

A Suggestion

Be prepared with a snappy answer for an offer of free cigarettes, such as

- "I can't afford to start smoking again."
- "Isn't it hard for you to promote cancer like this?"
- "Don't you know that cigarettes are bad for you?"
- "Do you smoke these?"

You can probably come up with an even better comeback of your own.

Tolerance

All addicting chemicals produce *tolerance*. Tolerance means that after many exposures to a chemical, brain cells resist the effects of the chemical. As a result of tolerance, addicted individuals must consume larger and larger amounts of the chemical to produce the same effect. Heroin, alcohol, cocaine—and nicotine—all produce tolerance. The development of tolerance indicates that the addictive process has begun. After quitting, tolerance drops temporarily, but it does not go away completely. This process happens with smokers (who are addicted to nicotine) just as it happens to individuals addicted to other drugs. When smokers relapse, the first cigarette makes them lightheaded, indicating that they have little tolerance; if they continue to smoke, however, tolerance quickly returns, and within a few days, they are usually smoking in their previous pattern.

A Step in the Right Direction

Did your first cigarette make you lightheaded? How long did it take for you to develop tolerance to one cigarette? This is the measure of when you first became dependent on nicotine. The maximum number of cigarettes you ever smoked in one day is a measure of how much tolerance you eventually developed; how high did your tolerance get before you finally quit smoking?

Be Aware of Threats to Your Recovery

Grocery stores and convenience stores display the "impulse buys" next to the cash register—candy, gum, magazines, and *cigarettes*. The store hopes that shoppers will pick up some of these items as they are waiting to check out and buy them, without paying attention. Impulse buying represents a relapse trigger for many recovering smokers, who may see their old brand of cigarettes on display and automatically buy a pack or a carton of them without realizing what they are doing. Once the cigarettes are home, it's very hard not to smoke them.

A Step in the Right Direction

You can help yourself avoid relapse by becoming more aware of what you buy and why you buy it. "Point-of-purchase" tobacco displays are bright, attractive, and frequently offer two-for-one "bargains," free merchandise, or other promotions to entice you. Can you smell the aroma of tobacco around the cigarette displays? Have you caught yourself automatically reaching out for a pack or carton of your old brand of cigarettes in the checkout line?

A Suggestion

The next time you see such a display, tell it, "Nice try, but I'm not falling for that sneaky trick."

Understanding Denial

Denial is the unconscious resistance to accepting the painful truth. When people are in denial, they cannot see or accept the truth about some aspect of their behavior. For example, a recent survey reported that 27 percent of registered nurses are smokers—in spite of the fact that every day, nurses see the death and disease caused by smoking. When they finally get clean and free, they relate that they simply did not connect their own smoking with the smoking-related illness of the patients they were treating. Denial is a serious barrier to recovery; half of all smokers die in denial.

A Step in the Right Direction

How can understanding your denial help you in your recovery?

A Suggestion

Think back to when you were a smoker in denial. Which "denial excuses" did you use when you were smoking? Are any of these familiar?

- "I know a guy who's seventy-five and he's been smoking all his life."
- "Lots of people who never smoked get cancer too."
- "No one ever robbed a gas station or mugged someone to get cigarettes."
- "Hey, you have to die from something, right?"

Do you hear active smokers making such statements? What do you tell them?

Impress Yourself

One of the most common reasons smokers give for deciding to quit smoking is to impress other people. Sometimes smokers decide to quit because other people have challenged them to or have doubted that they could. These reasons are *serious* enough for them to quit, but they may not be *personal* enough for them to recover.

A Step in the Right Direction

In order to recover—not just quit smoking—you must make your reasons more personal.

A Suggestion

Respond to the following questions in your journal.

- Who were you hoping to impress by becoming a smoker? What did it prove about you?
- Who do you hope to impress by quitting smoking? Why should that person care?
- If that person shows no interest in your recovery, will you start smoking again?
- If you quit smoking and no one noticed—no one at all—how would you feel?
- If you quit smoking and no one noticed, would you go back to smoking?
- Do your friends and family expect you to succeed or fail at quitting smoking?
- What does the fact that you have quit smoking prove about you today?

Time on Your Hands?

Smoking becomes a part of nearly everything that smokers do. They spend an average of two hours each day with their cigarettes—buying them, smoking them, and cleaning up after them. When they first quit smoking, they suddenly find that they have time on their hands. Most people quickly fill the time up with other activities and hardly notice the difference, but some never learn how to handle the extra time and return to smoking.

A Step in the Right Direction

Where in your day do you have extra time, now that you are no longer smoking?

- The time spent clearing out your lungs in the morning.
- The time you used to spend finding a place to smoke.
- The time you used to spend smoking (and not doing anything else).
- The time you wasted while smoking and doing something else at the same time.
- The time spent cleaning up after yourself.
- The time spent recovering from respiratory illnesses caused by smoking.

What are you filling this time with now? What would you tell smokers who are counting down to Quit Day about managing the extra time they will have after they quit?

Cigarettes Became Your Companion

Smokers develop a special relationship with their cigarettes. A year or so after they start smoking, smokers and their cigarettes become constant companions. Wherever smokers go, their cigarettes tag along. They go together to school, to work, out to dinner, to parties—everywhere. Some smokers won't even go out of the house without their cigarettes, and if they run out of cigarettes, they stop whatever they're doing to buy more. They might lose their keys or their hat, but they never lose their cigarettes.

A Step in the Right Direction

What kind of relationship did you develop with cigarettes? What was important to you about smoking? What did you get from smoking that you didn't get from anything else?

A Suggestion

Recall when you and your cigarettes started going places together. Choose one point in your life when you and your cigarettes were close companions. In your journal, list the places the two of you went together. Were there places you didn't take your cigarettes (such as church, to the doctor's office, or to the health club)? You and your cigarettes were once close companions, and as the years passed, you became closer and closer. Understanding your relationship with cigarettes and how it changed over the years will help you stay clean and free.

Making New Friends

Cigarettes control who smokers socialize with and who they have as friends. Smokers are often reluctant to quit because they know they will lose their connections with their smoking friends. As more and more people have quit smoking, smokers have bonded together more tightly, a threatened minority group. Recovering smokers often miss their old friends in the smoking group after they quit smoking—but they may no longer be welcome there. Early in their recovery, they may not yet have developed many friendships with nonsmokers. For some recovering smokers, this loss of belonging increases their risk of relapse. After all, the smokers will always be willing to take them back—if they start smoking again.

A Step in the Right Direction

When you were smoking, did you feel threatened by nonsmokers? Did you have a group of smoking friends that stuck together? Do you miss smoking with them? Hanging around your old smoking friends can endanger your recovery.

A Suggestion

You can improve your chances of staying clean and free by writing a "Good-bye" letter to tobacco. If you have already written one, pull it out, read it over, and add things that you have learned over the last month. If you have not written one, start today. Start with "Good-bye Tobacco," and tell tobacco why you are leaving it behind.

Eliminate Smoking Again as an Option

Many people quit smoking but secretly hope they will be able to smoke again one day. These thoughts may be conscious ("I'm waiting for them to invent a safe cigarette") or unconscious ("I don't want to smoke—I just keep these cigarettes around for guests who might want to smoke"). These smokers will probably return to smoking because they never made a total commitment to staying clean and free. They set *quitting* as their goal instead of *recovery.*

A Step in the Right Direction

Successful recovery from nicotine and tobacco dependence demands that you completely cut yourself off from any possibility of returning to smoking. Have you burned all the bridges behind you that lead back to smoking? If even one remains, you may use it to return to smoking in a moment of stress or temptation.

A Suggestion

Invest some time today to find out if you have broken your connections with your previous smoking behavior. Answer these questions in your journal:

- Have you thought that you could smoke again and keep it a secret?
- Do you have some cigarettes left in a place that no one knows about?
- If you found a pack of cigarettes in a drawer today, would you throw it out?

Smoking Changes Your Self-Image

People are exposed to tobacco messages from childhood on. Television carried cigarette ads until 1965; anyone who is older than forty-five saw quite a few of them. Today, people see billboards and magazine advertising featuring Joe Camel, the Marlboro Man, Virginia Slims women, and Kool guy every day. As a result, children learn that smoking is a rite of passage to adulthood; when they become smokers, they feel more mature. Adults learn that smokers are youthful, energetic people who have lots of fun and are popular with the opposite sex. Amazing! Children believe that smoking makes them older; adults believe that smoking keeps them young!

A Step in the Right Direction

When you were a young smoker, did smoking make you feel more mature? When you got older, did smoking make you feel more youthful?

A Suggestion

Describe in your journal one time during your childhood when smoking made you feel older and one time more recently when smoking made you feel more youthful. Now that you no longer smoke, do you feel older or younger?

Miserable Moments

Agatha Christie, the mystery writer, once wrote: "I like living. I have sometimes been wildly, despairingly, acutely miserable, racked with sorrow, but through it all I still knew quite certainly that just to be alive is a grand thing."

A Step in the Right Direction

Have you ever felt as depressed as Agatha Christie? Many recovering smokers become depressed after they quit smoking. Just giving up cigarettes is enough to make most smokers completely miserable. Have there been moments since you quit smoking when you said, "What's the use? I feel terrible and it's not getting any better—I might as well go back to smoking."

A Suggestion

Make a list of your most miserable moments since you quit smoking, and pair each one with a statement about your hope for the future. Here are some examples:

- Yesterday, I was craving a cigarette so bad I sat in the smoking section of the cafeteria and thought about picking some butts out of the ashtrays.
  - If I stick with this program, my obsessive thoughts will eventually go away.

- I frequently sit alone in the dark, and I think about . . . nothing.
  - Quitting smoking will give me the confidence to overcome my other problems.

Take Care of Yourself to Avoid Relapse

Fatigue can be a serious trigger to relapse for a recovering smoker. When people are deprived of sleep, overworked, or ill, their resistance drops. They become more like children: irritable, demanding, self-centered, and needy. But since they are adults, no one wants to treat them like children. That's when they may turn to their old friend who always gave everything and demanded nothing—their cigarettes.

A Step in the Right Direction

Since you quit smoking, have you had days when you were tired or worn out? Did you feel as if someone should be taking care of you? Did you start thinking about a cigarette?

A Suggestion

How is your energy level today? Many recovering smokers are in such a hurry to get everything done that they do not take good care of themselves. Allowing yourself to become fatigued puts you at risk for relapse. Look at the week ahead and find half an hour in each day to devote to resting and relaxing. This is the same half hour when you used to smoke, so you haven't really taken any time away from your schedule. Are you willing to rest a little more each day and take better care of yourself in order to improve your chances of staying clean and free?

Addiction Question Number 1

Dependence on nicotine and tobacco is an addiction, similar to alcohol dependence or cocaine dependence. Smokers are often reluctant to view smoking as an addiction, but it is an addiction. For the next week we will explore some of the addictive features of nicotine and tobacco by asking questions similar to those that addiction treatment specialists typically use to diagnose addictions.

A Step in the Right Direction

Today's question:

1. *Have you ever felt it was important to cut down or control your smoking?*

Addicts typically try to "control" their drug or alcohol use. If this works at all, it is usually for very brief periods. However, advocates of "controlled use" (of drugs, alcohol, or nicotine) are always popular with practicing addicts.

A Suggestion

Answer these questions with complete honesty.

- What symptoms did you have that made you decide to cut down or control your smoking? Why didn't you just quit smoking then?
- How did you try to keep your smoking under control (and not quit completely)?
- Did you manage to cut down temporarily but eventually return to smoking?

Addiction Question Number 2

This week we are looking at the addictive features of nicotine and tobacco by asking some of the questions addiction treatment specialists typically use to diagnose addictions, with the questions rephrased so they apply specifically to smoking.

A Step in the Right Direction

Today's question:

2. *Have you ever been annoyed or angry with someone who told you that you ought to quit smoking?*

Most smokers have at least a few people in their lives who want them to quit smoking. Smokers often react to these people with anger, resentment, and bitter words because they are not ready to admit that they should quit smoking.

A Suggestion

Answer these questions with complete honesty.

- During your years of smoking, how many people told you that you ought to quit smoking? What was your usual reaction?
- Did you get into arguments with people you care about over your smoking?
- Did you ever give up a friendship because smoking became an issue between you and your friend?

Addiction Question Number 3

We are examining the addictive aspects of smoking this week by asking questions similar to those that addiction treatment specialists typically use to diagnose addictions.

A Step in the Right Direction

Today's question:

3. *Have you ever felt guilty for something you did when you were smoking?*

People feel guilty when they know they've done something they shouldn't have done. Addicted smokers often choose their cigarettes over doing the right thing.

A Suggestion

Answer these questions with complete honesty.

- Did your smoking ever damage property? Did you tell the truth about the damage?
- Has anyone—particularly a child—ever been harmed by your cigarette smoke?
- Have you ever been so ashamed of being a smoker that you denied being one?
- Have you ever lied about how much you smoke to conceal how addicted you were?
- When you felt guilty about something, did you smoke to control these feelings?
- If someone had treated you the way you have treated your lungs, what would you have done?

Addiction Question Number 4

This week we are looking at the addictive features of dependence on nicotine and tobacco by asking the questions addiction treatment specialists typically use to diagnose addictions, with slight changes in the wording so the questions apply specifically to smoking.

A Step in the Right Direction

Today's question:

4. *Did you ever smoke first thing after waking up, to help you get started?*

Smoking right after waking up is evidence of severe nicotine dependence; the smoker needs a cigarette immediately to reverse the symptoms of nicotine withdrawal. Smoking upon awakening indicates that a smoker's thoughts, feelings, and behaviors are completely controlled by nicotine.

A Suggestion

Answer these questions with complete honesty.

- When you were smoking, how soon after you woke up did you smoke your first cigarette? Did you think about smoking as soon as you woke up?
- Did you have trouble thinking clearly before you smoked your first cigarette?
- Did you use cigarettes as a (legal) stimulant?
- Did you ever discover that you had run out of cigarettes first thing in the morning? If so, what did you do?

Addiction Question Number 5

We are examining the addictive aspects of smoking this week by asking some of the questions addiction treatment specialists use to diagnose addictions, with a few minor changes so the questions apply specifically to smoking.

A Step in the Right Direction

Today's question:

5. Have you ever compromised your values because of smoking?

What moral values are most important to you? Did you ever violate any of those values because of smoking?

A Suggestion

Answer these questions with complete honesty.

- Did you ever steal cigarettes?
- Did you ever smoke in a place where smoking was forbidden?
- Did you ever put off taking care of a child or a sick person until you finished your cigarette?
- Were you ever late for an appointment because you were smoking?
- Did you ever lie about your smoking?
- Did you ever claim to have quit smoking when you hadn't?
- What question about your smoking do you hope no one ever asks?

Addiction Question Number 6

This week we are looking at the addictive features of dependence on nicotine and tobacco by asking the questions addiction treatment specialists use to diagnose addictions, with the wording modified slightly so the questions apply specifically to smoking.

A Step in the Right Direction

Today's question:

6. *Did you ever change friends, jobs, or activities to avoid non-smoking people or because you couldn't smoke with those friends, at that job, or with those activities?*

When friends, jobs, and activities interfere with smoking, the smoker must make a choice. Recovering smokers must make these choices every day.

A Suggestion

Answer these questions with complete honesty.

- When you were smoking, were most of your friends also smokers?
- When one of your friends quit smoking, did he or she remain your friend?
- Did you ever choose a job because you could smoke at work? Did you ever leave a job because you couldn't?
- Did you ever choose a particular kind of recreation because you could smoke while you were doing it?

Addiction Question Number 7

Over the past six days, we have asked questions similar to those that addiction treatment specialists ask their patients about addictions.

A Step in the Right Direction

Today's question:

7. *Did you ever smoke when you were sick with a respiratory infection, allergies, or asthma (even though you knew it could make things worse)?*

Today you know that cigarettes cause much more physical damage than alcohol, cocaine, or heroin. You have probably known this fact for some time, but the knowledge alone was not enough to get you to quit.

A Suggestion

Answer these questions with complete honesty.

- When you were still smoking, did you know that smoking causes illness and death? What excuses did you make to yourself to justify your smoking?
- What physical damage has smoking done to you?
- How many of your respiratory illnesses has smoking caused over the years? Did it make some mild ones into serious ones?
- Have there been times when you smoked even though you were already sick with a respiratory illness?

Heal Your Skin with Guided Imagery

Use guided imagery to heal your damaged skin.

A Step in the Right Direction

Guided imagery is a valuable strategy for relaxing your body while focusing the power of your mind. Here is a guided imagery exercise you can use; you will find others as you move through this book.

Plan to do this exercise for about five minutes. Sit in a comfortable chair or lie down, legs and arms uncrossed. Close your eyes, and breathe slowly and deeply. With each deep breath, imagine yourself becoming more and more relaxed. Focus on your breathing. Continue to breathe deeply, allowing all the concerns of the day to leave your mind as the air leaves your lungs. When your body is thoroughly relaxed, turn your attention to the condition of the skin of your face. Notice the deep wrinkles caused by years of smoking. Focus the power of your mind on healing this damaged skin. Encourage the old, damaged cells to drop off, to be replaced by new, healthy cells from beneath. Feed these cells with nutrients from the blood vessels deeper in the skin. Continue to breathe deeply and relax. After about five minutes, open your eyes and notice how you feel.

A Suggestion

Use guided imagery every day to help your body and your mind heal.

Helping Others Quit

One of the most common reasons smokers give for deciding to quit smoking is to be supportive of other people's efforts to quit smoking. This reason is *serious* enough for them to quit, but it may not be *personal* enough for them to recover.

A Step in the Right Direction

In order to recover—not just quit smoking—you must make your reasons more personal.

A Suggestion

Respond to the following questions in your journal.

- How will your recovery improve someone else's chances of quitting?
- Does someone else's recovery depend on you staying clean and free?
- Is it important to you, as a newly recovering smoker, to be a nonsmoking role model for someone else?
- Have you tried to help other people quit smoking, only to discover that your interest in their recovery was greater than theirs?
- Have you endangered your own recovery by trying to help someone else quit smoking? How would you feel if your effort to help someone else resulted in your relapse?

Smoking Causes Heart Disease

Smoking leads to over 400,000 deaths in America every year, according to the surgeon general. About 25 percent of these deaths are due to coronary heart disease. The coronary arteries carry blood to the heart, providing it with oxygen and nutrients. Deposits of fat and cholesterol can block these arteries, preventing the blood from reaching the heart muscle. When the blockage becomes severe, the person has a heart attack—part of the heart muscle actually dies. Fifty percent of all heart attack victims die on the spot. Smoking is one of many causes of heart disease; other causes include high blood pressure, a diet high in fat and cholesterol, obesity, and heredity. People can't change their hereditary risk of heart disease, but they can change other risk factors—especially smoking.

A Step in the Right Direction

Have you been concerned about getting heart disease? Have you known someone who did? Here's the good news: now that you have quit smoking, your risk of having a heart attack will gradually decrease, and in about five years, it will drop to the same risk as the rest of the population.

A Suggestion

Take a good look at your overall health. Now that you are not smoking, what other changes are you considering to improve your health?

Good to the Last Drop?

Drinking a cup of coffee is an automatic signal to smoke a cigarette for many people. Recent research shows that the link between coffee and nicotine may be biochemical, as well as psychological. These factors combine to make most smokers associate the aroma and flavor of coffee with smoking. Smokers associate smoking with the first cup of coffee in the morning, with coffee breaks, with coffee at meals, and with coffee and dessert. For some recovering smokers, the aroma and flavor of brewing coffee automatically divert their thinking to smoking, even months after their last cigarette.

A Step in the Right Direction

Did you frequently smoke a cigarette with coffee? Was your coffee break really a coffee-and-cigarette break? Did you frequently smoke with coffee first thing in the morning, or after a meal? What can you do to eliminate the aroma and flavor of coffee as a relapse trigger?

A Suggestion

Try switching to a beverage other than coffee for a little while. Drinking the first cup of coffee in the morning, coffee breaks at work, and coffee after dinner at a restaurant are examples of high-risk situations for many recovering smokers. Would it be worth giving up the satisfaction of a cup of coffee for a while if it helps you stay clean and free?

Having the Courage to Change

Change is threatening to most people. Even when they are having problems, most people don't want to change. "The devil you know is better than the devil you don't know," they say. They stay in abusive relationships, remain overweight, stay in jobs they hate, and pretend to like people they despise, all because making changes is too hard. Change means risking insecurity, frustration, and anxiety.

A Step in the Right Direction

Years before you actually quit, you knew that smoking was bad for you. Why were you afraid to change? What was it about the idea of life without cigarettes that made it so hard to make a decision to change? What finally convinced you to change? Some recovering smokers can identify a specific moment in their lives when they decided to quit. Since you quit smoking, have you occasionally thought that it wasn't such a good idea after all?

A Suggestion

On an index card or the back of a business card, write a note that will remind you of the benefits of not smoking. Carry this card (or a Quit Card) with you every day for a week, and refer to it often. If you start having doubts about the value of being clean and free, pull out your card and read the message.

Health Warnings

In 1964, the U.S. Congress required tobacco companies to include health information warnings on each pack of cigarettes and in each advertisement. The original warning, "The Surgeon General has determined that cigarette smoking may be hazardous to your health," seems tame compared to the current warnings:

- "Surgeon General's Warning: Cigarette Smoke Contains Carbon Monoxide."
- "Smoking Causes Lung Cancer, Heart Disease, Emphysema and May Complicate Pregnancy."
- "Quitting Smoking Now Greatly Reduces Serious Risks to Your Health."

These warnings are printed in small letters on the sides of cigarette packs and in smaller letters in cigarette ads. The Canadian warnings are even stronger, requiring messages such as "Cigarettes cause strokes and heart disease" and "Cigarettes cause fatal lung disease" to be printed in bold letters on each pack of cigarettes—in both English and French.

A Step in the Right Direction

Did you ever notice the health warnings before? How do these warnings apply to you?

A Suggestion

Write a few cigarette warnings of your own. Exactly what should people know about cigarettes before they smoke them?

Nicotine Anonymous

Nicotine Anonymous is a support group for people who want to quit smoking. It is patterned after Alcoholics Anonymous and relies on many of the same principles. There are no dues or fees, there are no requirements for membership, and there are no paid leaders. Nicotine Anonymous provides support for people who want to remain clean and free, and it emphasizes the spiritual aspects of recovery. Nicotine Anonymous meetings usually last one hour; books and pamphlets describing the program are available at these meetings. Many people value the group support so much that they continue to attend meetings long after they have smoked their last cigarette.

A Step in the Right Direction

Can Nicotine Anonymous help *you?* Even if you are not the kind of person who feels comfortable in groups, you may find that the people at Nicotine Anonymous can help you avoid relapse. At this point in your recovery, you need all the help you can get.

A Suggestion

You do not have to make any commitment to the organization by attending a meeting. So, if you have never attended one, why not go once and see what it's like? To find the location of a meeting in your area, call their central office in San Francisco at (415) 750-0328.

Some Weight Gain Is Normal

The fear of gaining weight is one of the reasons smokers hesitate to quit. Weight gain becomes a serious problem for many people when they quit smoking, and it is a legitimate concern. However, not everyone who quits smoking gains weight, and of those who do, the average is about eight pounds. Some smoking cessation counselors work hard to help people quit smoking without gaining weight by giving them special diets or exercise programs. Recent research, however, shows that individuals who gained a little weight had better success in quitting smoking than those who struggled to keep their weight the same. This research suggests that working hard at dieting distracts recovering smokers from dealing with their smoking.

A Step in the Right Direction

Which would you prefer: to quit smoking and gain a few pounds or to continue smoking and weigh the same? Is this a difficult choice for you?

A Suggestion

Put the bathroom scale away for a couple of months. You have already decided that your life will be better and you will live longer by quitting smoking; are you willing to tolerate gaining a few pounds if it improves your chances of staying clean and free? You may not look like the models in the cigarette ads, but you will be healthier.

Dealing with Bad News

Receiving bad news is often the event that triggers a recovering smoker to relapse. A death in the family, a serious problem at work, a conflict with a loved one, a child getting into trouble—these events may cause more stress than the recovering smoker knows how to handle. Recovering smokers can't eliminate stress from their lives, but they can learn how to cope with it, and most important, how to cope without smoking.

A Step in the Right Direction

When you were still smoking, how did you deal with bad news? Did you smoke to help you cope? How have you dealt with bad news since you quit smoking? Did you act impulsively, without thinking what the results of your actions would be? Or did you calmly think ahead and plan your actions?

A Suggestion

The next time you receive bad news, don't act right away. Instead, say the Serenity Prayer to yourself, over and over, until you know what to do:

> *God, grant me the serenity*
> *to accept the things I cannot change,*
> *the courage to change the things I can,*
> *and the wisdom to know the difference.*

What are some of the things in life you need to accept? What are some of the things you need to change?

Relapse Rates Are Very High

Research shows that 95 percent of teenage smokers try to quit smoking within five years of graduating from high school, but only 25 percent of them are able to quit. An analysis of thirty-nine smoking cessation research projects showed that of all the people who quit smoking in these studies, 25 percent started smoking again in two days, and half started smoking again within a week. At the end of twelve months, only 12 percent were still smokefree.

A Step in the Right Direction

Smokers *stop smoking* all the time—you stopped smoking every time you crushed out a cigarette (and until you lit the next one). *Quitting smoking* means making a commitment to not start again. Research shows, however, that relapse rates are extremely high in people who have quit smoking.

A Suggestion

Set *recovery* as your goal instead of quitting. Recovery means that you have fully accepted your nicotine and tobacco dependence, that you understand how you relied on cigarettes, and that smoking again is no longer an option for you. You can improve the quality of your recovery by working on understanding your addiction and yourself every single day. What will you do today to improve the quality of your recovery?

An Easier, Softer Way

After not smoking for two or three months, some recovering smokers are tempted to use smokeless tobacco. They reason that smokeless tobacco doesn't cause lung cancer, and since they don't really like smokeless tobacco, they won't use much of it. Conversely, some smokeless tobacco users think they can safely smoke cigarettes. They reason that cigarettes don't cause as much gum damage and mouth cancer as smokeless tobacco does, and since they don't really like smoking, they won't smoke much. Cigarette smokers consider switching to a pipe; pipe smokers think about switching to cigars; cigar smokers try switching to cigarettes. All these efforts to control nicotine and tobacco use will fail because switchers are still users, and they usually return to their drug of choice—cigarettes, cigars, a pipe, or smokeless tobacco.

A Step in the Right Direction

Have you thought about switching to another form of tobacco instead of quitting? Some alcoholics try to control their drinking by switching from whiskey to beer; in AA, this is referred to as looking for an "easier, softer way," and it never works.

A Suggestion

Remind yourself that *any* form of tobacco is a threat to your life, your health, and your self-esteem. Clean and free means clean and free from *all* forms of tobacco.

Your Attitudes about Smoking Have Changed

Attitudes control behavior. Attitudes change very slowly; some persist over a person's entire lifetime. Psychologists have learned that attitudes change more quickly when behavior changes first; people tend to change their attitudes to match their new behavior. Their new attitudes then affect future behavior. For example, most smokers believe that they should be allowed to smoke wherever they want and that the tobacco companies should be allowed to sell their products with minimal regulation. After quitting smoking (a new behavior), these attitudes begin to change.

A Step in the Right Direction

How have your attitudes about smokers and smoking changed since you quit smoking? Have you also changed your attitudes about the tobacco companies that took your money for so many years? Your attitudes have changed because your behavior has changed: you are no longer smoking. You no longer need to give nicotine and tobacco control over your thoughts, feelings, and attitudes.

A Suggestion

Express your new attitudes about cigarettes, smoking, smokers, and the tobacco companies in constructive ways. Use your experiences to become a positive role model for other smokers who have been trying to quit smoking.

What Does "Relapse" Mean?

Almost 90 percent of smokers who quit smoking start again before a year is up. This event is called a "relapse." But relapses usually begin long before the recovering smoker takes that first puff—they begin when it becomes *possible* to smoke again. The first puff is just a part of the relapse process; its beginning may have been days or weeks earlier. A relapse may start when the recovering smoker starts going on coffee breaks with a group of smokers; eventually, he or she will accept a cigarette. A relapse may start when the recovering smoker lingers over the display of cigarettes at the grocery checkout counter; soon, he or she will buy a pack.

A Step in the Right Direction

Staying clean and free depends on recognizing when you are drifting toward relapse. Relapse is like a whirlpool—if you keep making forward progress, you can swim right through it; but if you stop swimming and allow yourself to drift, it will slowly capture you, sucking you in, drowning you before you realize what has happened. To avoid being a victim, you must stay alert and recognize the danger signs of relapse.

A Suggestion

Identify ten situations you will be in this next week where smoking again would be possible. How will you protect yourself in these situations?

This Brand's for You

The tobacco companies have tried to fill every possible "market niche." They have cigarettes for men (Camel, Chesterfield), for women (Virginia Slims, Capri), for African Americans (Newport), for individualists (Marlboro), for untraditional smokers (Dave's), for sophisticated people (Benson and Hedges), for thrifty smokers (Doral, Basic), and for those who are concerned about their health (Carlton, True). They have regular-strength cigarettes, medium-strength cigarettes, light cigarettes, and ultralight cigarettes. The models in their ads are selected to appeal to risk-taking young adults (the Marlboro Adventure Team), to trendy twentysomethings (Kool), and to kids who watch Saturday morning cartoons (Joe Camel). In spite of what the advertising says, the tobacco and the nicotine in all cigarettes are essentially the same, and there is no evidence that any brand of cigarette is safer than others.

A Step in the Right Direction

What attracted you to the brand you used to smoke? Tobacco companies would like you to start smoking again. What image might attract you back to smoking?

A Suggestion

In your journal, describe why you once identified with the image created by the tobacco companies of a smoker of your old brand of cigarettes.

Becoming a Nonsmoker

Smokers tend to associate with other smokers, and nonsmokers tend to associate with other nonsmokers. Smokers stand outside and smoke together, share cigarettes and lights with each other, and complain about having limits placed on where they can smoke. Nonsmokers rarely talk about *not* smoking, but when they see smokers gather together to smoke, they often wonder why anyone would want to pollute their lungs with tobacco smoke. Smokers frequently feel resentful toward nonsmokers for banning smoking in public places, and nonsmokers feel resentful toward smokers who smoke near them. Smokers think about smoking twenty or thirty or more times each day; nonsmokers hardly ever think about smoking.

A Step in the Right Direction

Are you more comfortable being a smoker or being a nonsmoker? Today, you are in transition from being a smoker to being a nonsmoker. What will be the most difficult part of joining the nonsmokers?

A Suggestion

Make a list of the things you will miss most about being a smoker. Then make a list of the things you will value most about being a nonsmoker. What will you have to do to be accepted by the nonsmokers as one of them?

Use Your Imagination

When recovering smokers think about smoking, they often fantasize about the pleasures of smoking. Such fantasies can be relapse triggers.

A Step in the Right Direction

There are many wonderful things about smoking—the lift that nicotine gave you, the satisfaction of having something to do with your hands, the relaxation of sucking in the smoke and blowing it out. There is no doubt that smoking made you feel good. You decided to quit smoking because the damage done by cigarettes outweighed the pleasure of smoking. When you start reminiscing about the pleasures of smoking, it means that you are closer to a relapse.

A Suggestion

You can take action against relapse. Every time you have a positive thought about smoking, immediately counter it by recalling an unpleasant memory that relates to the pleasant one. For instance, if you love to recall inhaling deeply on a cigarette first thing in the morning, force yourself to recall how you coughed and choked immediately afterward. If you start thinking about being on vacation at the beach and lazily smoking a cigarette, force yourself to recall being so sick with bronchitis that you couldn't go to work.

Recreation Can Remind You of Smoking

Cigarettes infiltrate themselves into every aspect of smokers' lives, including their hobbies, sports, and leisure activities. Without being aware of it, smokers choose recreation that permits smoking and friends who also smoke. They choose outdoor sports over indoor ones (hunting, gardening) so they can smoke; sports with periods of inactivity (bowling, softball) so they can smoke; and sports that do not require all-out exertion (fishing, boating) because smoking has damaged their lungs. After quitting, these hobbies, sports, and other kinds of recreation can become triggers for relapse.

A Step in the Right Direction

Which recreation and leisure activities did you like to do when you were a smoker? How was smoking a part of them? Since you quit smoking, have you been reminded of smoking while doing these activities? Your old hobbies and sports activities may be strong reminders of smoking right now; you may need to avoid them for a while.

A Suggestion

Identify some recreational and leisure-time activities that you have never associated with smoking. Choose one that appeals to you, and check it out this week.

Cigarettes Betrayed You

Cigarettes become a dedicated smoker's best friend. They are consistent, reliable, and always available. They never disagree or talk back; they ask nothing and give everything. What a terrific friend! Smokers love them, trust them, and protect them—and in return, cigarettes give them lung disease, cancer, strokes, and heart damage. And yet, most smokers are reluctant to abandon their old friend.

A Step in the Right Direction

Wouldn't it be great if all your friends were as consistent, reliable, and available as your cigarettes once were? What were some of the good times the two of you had together? How did you rely on them? It's normal to miss an old friend and to recall the good times you shared, but dwelling too long on the "good old days" will put you at risk for relapse. Cigarettes were once your friend, but then they started to steal your breath, sap your strength, and fill your body with poisons.

A Suggestion

Identify (if you can) the event that finally convinced you to quit smoking. How did you feel when you finally accepted that cigarettes had betrayed your trust and that they were no longer your friend?

Heal Your Stomach with Guided Imagery

Use guided imagery to improve the condition of your stomach.

A Step in the Right Direction

Guided imagery is a valuable strategy for relaxing your body while focusing the power of your mind. Here is a guided imagery exercise you can use; you will find others as you move through the *Keep Quit* program.

Plan to do this exercise for about five minutes. Sit in a comfortable chair or lie down, legs and arms uncrossed. Close your eyes, and breathe slowly and deeply. With each deep breath, imagine yourself becoming more and more relaxed. Focus on your breathing. Continue to breathe deeply, allowing all the concerns of the day to leave your mind as the air leaves your lungs. When your body is thoroughly relaxed, turn your attention to the inside of your stomach. Toxic chemicals in tobacco smoke have irritated and eroded the lining of your stomach. Search for shallow holes oozing blood and mucus; these are ulcers. Now search for areas that look like they have been scraped with sandpaper; these areas are in danger of becoming ulcers. Focus the power of your mind on healing these damaged areas. Continue to breathe deeply and relax. After about five minutes, open your eyes and notice how you feel.

A Suggestion

Use guided imagery every day to help your body and your mind heal.

Identify Yourself as a Nonsmoker

Recovering smokers are often tempted to smoke when smokers offer them a cigarette. Making plans to deal with such situations before they occur improves a recovering smoker's chances of staying clean and free.

A Step in the Right Direction

Many smokers feel guilty because they know they should stop smoking, but they haven't been willing to put out the effort. Your recovery reminds them of their inadequacy. Since they can't stop, they may try to get *you* to start smoking again. One day someone may offer you a cigarette, saying, "I don't like to smoke alone—please, have one with me." If you are the kind of person who hates to disappoint people, this manipulation may hook you and you may accept a cigarette even if you don't really want one. Could this situation be a relapse trigger for you? How would you answer the person offering you a cigarette?

A Suggestion

Consider saying, "Sorry, I'm a nonsmoker now. I used to think I couldn't quit, but I've learned that I can—and I'd be glad to tell you how I did it." Not many smokers will take you up on your offer, but at least they will stop offering you cigarettes. What other good responses have you thought of?

Denial Is a Barrier to Recovery

Denial is a defense against the truth when the truth is too difficult to accept. People do not give up their denial willingly. Smokers in denial say, "I feel fine—smoking hasn't done anything to me." They ignore the warning signs of disease and become defensive when others criticize their smoking or suggest that they quit smoking. Denial is *unconscious,* so a smoker in denial cannot be convinced to change by logic; smokers in denial frequently react to caring and logical advice with anger and hostility. It takes a long time for them to break through their denial and finally accept that they have a problem. Many never do.

A Step in the Right Direction

When you were smoking, how deep was your denial? How can understanding denial help you stay clean and free?

A Suggestion

Recall when you were a smoker in denial.

- Did you get angry or hostile when others suggested you quit smoking?
- Did you hide your smoking from people and tell them you weren't smoking?
- Did you insist that your cough or chest pains were unrelated to your smoking?
- Did you become defensive when you were with a recovering smoker?

Make some notes in your journal about your own experiences with denial.

Dreaming Increases in Early Recovery

Dreams are a natural part of sleep; they occur every ninety minutes or so throughout the night and are associated with rapid back-and-forth movements of the eyes beneath closed lids. Scientists call these episodes REM (rapid eye movement) sleep. Dreaming sleep is disrupted by addicting drugs, especially alcohol, Valium, cocaine, marijuana—and nicotine. In early recovery from addiction to these drugs, there is usually an increase in the intensity and frequency of dreams, called "REM rebound." These dreams may be vivid and threatening; they are often about using the chemical, and the dreamer may awaken believing the dream was real. The dreams often recur, night after night. Since many of these dreams are disturbing and interrupt sleep, people often want to stop having them; however, REM rebound appears to be the way the brain readjusts itself to being without chemicals. REM rebound cannot be avoided and shouldn't be; it means that your brain is healing.

A Step in the Right Direction

Have you dreamed about smoking?

A Suggestion

Capture your dreams in order to understand them better. Keep a pencil and paper by your bedside; as soon as you are awakened by a dream, write down as much as you can remember about it. Later, see what you can learn about your recovery from recalling your dreams.

Taking Action

Relapses are common in all addictions, including nicotine and tobacco dependence. After a relapse, many relapsed smokers put off the decision to quit smoking again. They may say they *want* to quit again, and they may say they *intend* to quit again, but they delay taking *action*. It's much easier for them to keep on smoking—after all, smoking is much more familiar than not smoking. However, the longer a relapsed smoker continues to smoke, the more difficult it becomes to quit again. Many continue to smoke until they get a serious medical complication of smoking—and even then, many do not quit.

A Step in the Right Direction

Do you understand why relapsed smokers often delay quitting again? Research shows that when relapsed smokers put off quitting again, their nicotine and tobacco dependence becomes more intense with each cigarette they smoke. However, their chances of getting clean and free improve if they *immediately* begin work on quitting again. How could you help a relapsed smoker take action quickly? Share with this person how *you* made the decision to quit smoking. Like most people, relapsed smokers usually reject advice, but they will accept suggestions from someone who has had similar personal experiences.

Look to the Future

Relapses are common in all addictions, including nicotine and tobacco dependence. When recovering smokers relapse, they often discount the progress they have made because they are smoking again. They may say, "Now I have to start all over again." But they are not really starting all over again. They learned a great deal about recovery during the days, weeks, or months when they were clean and free. They know more than they think they do about what works and what doesn't, and about how their lives can be different. They often have trouble accepting praise for what they *have done* and want to focus only on what they *have not* done.

A Step in the Right Direction

Do you know one or more recovering smokers who have relapsed? Are they beating themselves up over the past? If so, they are in danger of throwing away everything they have accomplished because of their embarrassment and shame at relapsing. How can you help them look to the future instead of the past?

A Suggestion

Point out the progress they made before their relapse, help them see what was working for them, and help them identify when they began drifting toward relapse. Which *Keep Quit* strategies might help them overcome their barriers to success?

A Clean Break with Tobacco

Many people quit smoking but do not make a commitment to recovery. Many cling to the hope that one day a "safe" cigarette will be invented. Many smokers quit but secretly expect to smoke again some day—when they retire, when they reach a certain age, or if they come down with a fatal illness. Surveys indicate that teenage smokers often quit smoking and start again in a few months, believing that they will quit again soon. A few smokers switch to smokeless tobacco, believing that they will no longer be at risk of diseases caused by tobacco. None of these people have made a clean break with tobacco, leaving them all at a high risk for relapse.

A Step in the Right Direction

Have you made a clean break with tobacco or have you secretly thought that you will probably go back to smoking some day? What would make it all right for you to smoke again? In order to stay clean and free, you must make a clean break with tobacco.

A Suggestion

Writing a "Good-bye" letter to tobacco is a step in the right direction. If you have already written one, pull it out, read it over, and add things that you have learned about yourself in the last month. If you have not written one, start today. Start with "Good-bye Tobacco," and tell tobacco why you have left it behind.

Moments of Difficulty

Most smokers are not aware of how many purposes they use their cigarettes for. Smoking helps people deal with boredom, lapses in conversation, and being at a loss for words. Cigarettes give smokers something to focus on when they want to avoid answering a question, or when they just want to buy a little time. After quitting, recovering smokers no longer have cigarettes to hide behind, and this can create problems if they are not prepared. Knowing when and how they used cigarettes prepares them to deal with these situations in recovery.

A Step in the Right Direction

When did you use cigarettes? Many recovering smokers say, "I don't know—I smoked *all the time*." But no one smokes all the time; people smoke at many specific times that seem to run together. These events are like a drumroll—a drumroll appears to be a continuous sound, but it is really dozens of individual drumbeats.

A Suggestion

Keep track of the "moments of difficulty" you have during the next two days, such as when someone disappoints you, when you have a disagreement with someone, or when you misplace something. You will discover that there are dozens of such moments in every day. When you were still smoking, did you turn to a cigarette in moments like these? Since you are no longer smoking, how are you dealing with these situations?

Confront the Tobacco Companies

Tobacco companies spend millions of dollars every year creating an image for each of their products. They want people to think of smoking as an "adult custom," not as an addiction. They want people to think of cigarettes as a normal part of having a good time, not as the cause of cancer and heart disease. They could not do this without advertising and promotions, designed to lure teenagers and recovering smokers into picking up a cigarette.

A Step in the Right Direction

How were you and millions of others manipulated by tobacco companies to use their products? Through their financial support, the tobacco companies also manipulate organizations such as the NAACP, the National Rifle Association, the Republican Party, and the Democratic Party. The tobacco companies exhibit at their conventions, buy advertisements in their journals, and make contributions to their political campaigns.

A Suggestion

Does an organization you belong to accept support from the tobacco companies? You can do something about this. Write to the leaders of your organization and tell them why they should not support the tobacco industry.

Psychological Benefits of Smoking

All smokers do not receive the same psychological advantages from smoking. Research shows that smokers tend to smoke for one or more of these six reasons: chemical stimulation, having something to handle, tension reduction, pleasurable relaxation, craving, or habit. The benefit received from each aspect of smoking varies with each smoker. In the next week, we will look in more detail at each of these six psychological advantages of smoking.

A Step in the Right Direction

What were the psychological advantages you got from smoking? When you were smoking, you may not have been aware of these psychological advantages—smokers rarely are. Now you have quit smoking. How can understanding the psychological benefits of smoking help you stay clean and free?

A Suggestion

Consider each of the six psychological benefits of smoking and rate their importance to you when you were smoking. Write them down in order of importance in your journal. This is important, because the advantages you miss the most represent relapse triggers for you, and if you smoke just one cigarette, the chances are high that you will resume regular daily smoking.

Psychological Benefits of Smoking Number 1

Researchers classify the psychological benefits of smoking into these six categories: chemical stimulation, having something to handle, tension reduction, pleasurable relaxation, craving, and habit. Today, we will look at *chemical stimulation.*

Some smokers use cigarettes primarily to get started in the morning, to sharpen their concentration, to perk themselves up, or to combat fatigue. These people are responding to the mind- and mood-altering effects of the chemical nicotine, which are similar to those of cocaine and amphetamines. When they quit smoking, these people may feel depressed, lethargic, and discouraged; their energy level may be so low that they have trouble getting through the day.

A Step in the Right Direction

Did you smoke for the chemical stimulation from nicotine? If so, you are in danger of substituting other stimulants for nicotine, such as caffeine and sugar. This may lead you back to regular daily smoking. What healthy alternative can you use in place of the stimulant effect of nicotine?

A Suggestion

Start a morning exercise program. Ask a trainer at a health club for advice about starting slowly and increasing your exercise gradually. Now that you're not smoking, you will be able to exercise more easily. Starting an exercise program—and sticking with it—can help you stay clean and free.

Psychological Benefits of Smoking Number 2

Researchers classify the psychological benefits of smoking into these six categories: chemical stimulation, having something to handle, tension reduction, pleasurable relaxation, craving, and habit. Today, we will look at *handling*.

Some smokers use cigarettes primarily because they enjoy doing things with their cigarettes. They develop complex and very personal rituals around their smoking. They carry the pack in a certain place; they open the pack and pull out a cigarette in a certain way. They have a special way of lighting, holding, and puffing on a cigarette; they have their own way of flicking off the ash and putting the cigarette out when they are done. These rituals help the smoker feel secure and comfortable.

A Step in the Right Direction

Did you smoke because of the satisfaction of having something to handle? If so, you are at risk for relapse because you will probably miss all the things you used to do with a cigarette. This may lead you back to regular daily smoking. What can you do to avoid this cause of relapse?

A Suggestion

Find other things to handle in place of cigarettes. Always have a pen, a pencil, a plastic stirstick, a paper clip, or a rubber band with you. When you feel like holding a cigarette, play with your substitute instead. In time, your need for handling will decrease.

Psychological Benefits of Smoking Number 3

Researchers classify the psychological benefits of smoking into these six categories: chemical stimulation, having something to handle, tension reduction, pleasurable relaxation, craving, and habit. Today, we will look at *tension reduction*.

Anxiety and tension are a part of everyday life, but some people are more bothered by tension than others are. Many smokers use tobacco and nicotine to deal with tension. Their bodies react to tension with an increase in heart rate and blood pressure, and their muscles tighten up; they may wring their hands, clench their teeth, and crack their knuckles, trying to deal with the tension. They use cigarettes to reduce the tension and they discover that it works better than anything else.

A Step in the Right Direction

Did you smoke to reduce tension? If so, you are in danger of relapse whenever you are in a situation that makes you feel tense—which could be every day. This may lead you back to regular daily smoking. What can you do to avoid relapsing because of tension?

A Suggestion

Learn some new techniques that you can use when you feel tense, techniques such as relaxation exercises and guided imagery. (Check the index for relaxation exercises and imagery.) If you practice these exercises regularly, you will become skilled at them.

Psychological Benefits of Smoking Number 4

Researchers classify the psychological benefits of smoking into these six categories: chemical stimulation, having something to handle, tension reduction, pleasurable relaxation, craving, and habit. Today, we will look at *pleasurable relaxation.*

Many smokers use cigarettes primarily to enhance good feelings. They enjoy a cigarette after a meal, while watching TV, when drinking alcohol, after having sex, while playing cards, and at parties. These people associate cigarettes with good times.

A Step in the Right Direction

Did you smoke to relax and enjoy yourself? If so, you are in danger of relapse whenever you are at a party, spending time with friends, relaxing on the beach, or are in other enjoyable situations. This may lead you back to regular daily smoking. What can you do to avoid relapsing when you are relaxing or having fun?

A Suggestion

Make a list of the fun activities you associate with smoking. For the first year after quitting smoking, rearrange your recreational time to avoid places where smoking is encouraged (bars, nightclubs, and the homes of smokers); socialize only with nonsmoking friends; and do not allow visitors to smoke in your home. Are you willing to give up some fun things for a while so you can stay clean and free?

Psychological Benefits of Smoking Number 5

Researchers classify the psychological benefits of smoking into these six categories: chemical stimulation, having something to handle, tension reduction, pleasurable relaxation, craving, and habit. Today, we will look at *craving.*

Craving is more than wanting a cigarette; it is closer to a "drive" like breathing. Addicted smokers who are craving a cigarette don't just want one, they *need* one. They will do amazing things to get a cigarette; then they explain their actions by saying, "I didn't have any choice—the craving was more than I could stand."

A Step in the Right Direction

Did you smoke because of your craving for a cigarette? If so, you are at risk of relapse whenever something reminds you of smoking. This may lead you back to regular daily smoking. What can you do to avoid relapsing because of craving?

A Suggestion

Make a list of the most irrational things you ever did to obtain or use cigarettes, such as driving twenty miles out of your way to find a store that sold them, or smoking where you could have caused a fire. How did you explain or justify your actions in those situations? Did you have any options besides smoking? Understanding craving can help you stay clean and free. As a recovering smoker, what would you tell a smoker whose craving seemed overwhelming in situations similar to the ones you have described?

Psychological Benefits of Smoking Number 6

Researchers classify the psychological benefits of smoking into these six categories: chemical stimulation, having something to handle, tension reduction, pleasurable relaxation, craving, and habit. Today, we will look at *habit.*

Some smokers can take a cigarette out of the pack, light it, and smoke it without even thinking about it. They can smoke an entire pack without being aware of smoking more than a few cigarettes. This is called *automatic smoking.*

A Step in the Right Direction

Did you smoke without even thinking about it? If so, you are at risk of relapse whenever you start taking your recovery from nicotine and tobacco dependence for granted. Taking your recovery for granted may lead you back to smoking. What can you do to avoid relapsing because of habit?

A Suggestion

The next time you are with a smoker, watch how many things that person does with his or her cigarette without even thinking. Now pay attention to the things *you* do without thinking. Which actions are somehow connected to your old smoking behaviors? To stay clean and free, you must recognize your own *automatic behaviors.* If you don't, you could easily relapse without really intending to. For example, you could pick up someone else's cigarette at a party or a restaurant and smoke it, forgetting for the moment that you have quit smoking.

Psychological Benefits of Smoking

During this week, we have looked at the six primary psychological benefits people get from smoking: chemical stimulation, having something to handle, tension reduction, pleasurable relaxation, craving, and habit.

A Step in the Right Direction

How does understanding the benefits you got from smoking help you stay clean and free?

A Suggestion

Review the previous six pages in this book, which discuss the six primary psychological benefits of smoking. Give each psychological benefit a score from zero to five, based on the level of satisfaction it gave you when you were smoking. Most people score some benefits high and others low; others score them all about the same. Based on your scores, which areas do you need to focus on in order to stay clean and free? Consider these brief suggestions.

- *Stimulation.* Find new ways to keep alert, such as increasing your exercise.
- *Handling.* Keep your hands busy with a pencil, paper clip, or toothpick.
- *Tension.* Learn new ways to deal with stress, such as relaxation techniques.
- *Pleasurable relaxation.* Change your leisure activities to avoid smoking situations.
- *Craving.* Study how cigarettes made you act irrationally.
- *Habit.* Observe the automatic behaviors of others and pay attention to your own.

What Is Your Opinion?

Relapses don't just happen. Even when recovering smokers relapse "suddenly," signs that a relapse was impending can usually be found. When these smokers look carefully, they can see when their thoughts and feelings, behavior, and attitudes began to change—but the change was so gradual that most people (including themselves) never noticed. Many relapses can be prevented by recognizing the subtle signs of an impending relapse. Often other people can see these signs more easily than the recovering smoker can—signs like increasing irritability, minimizing the damage done by smoking, paying more attention to smokers, and defending the tobacco companies. Unfortunately, part of the relapse process is an unwillingness to listen to the opinions of other people, people who might be able to see the relapse coming.

A Step in the Right Direction

Do you think you are in danger of relapsing? Are you willing to listen to the opinions of others who might know?

A Suggestion

Ask someone you really trust how you are doing in your recovery. Then ask that person if he or she sees anything you are doing that could put you at risk for relapse. Write down what you are told in your journal and read it over several times. Does it make sense? Would you be willing to take some advice you don't really want in order to stay clean and free?

Effective Treatment for Depression

Some people become depressed after they quit smoking. Research has shown that depressed people are more likely to become smokers than nondepressed people, that depressed smokers have a harder time quitting than nondepressed smokers, and that recovering smokers who are depressed relapse more often than recovering smokers who are not depressed. Part of the explanation for these findings is that nicotine has antidepressant properties—many depressed smokers are actually medicating their depression by smoking. However, depression can be more effectively treated with psychotherapy, antidepressant medication, or a combination of both. Once under treatment, a person with depression usually improves in a few weeks. With so many good treatments available, there is no reason for a person to suffer with depression.

A Step in the Right Direction

Have you felt depressed (not just unhappy, angry, or frustrated) since you quit smoking? The symptoms of depression include crying spells, a feeling of hopelessness, loss of interest in doing things you used to enjoy, thoughts of harming yourself or thoughts of suicide, having hallucinations or intrusive thoughts, a change in appetite, and difficulty sleeping. Have you developed any of these symptoms since you quit smoking? If so, discuss them with your doctor, counselor, or therapist.

Billboards Are Persuasive

The tobacco companies spend over $3.5 billion each year to promote their products; a substantial proportion of that amount goes for billboards. Billboards must be bold, colorful, and persuasive, since motorists only look at them for a second or two. Typical billboard ads show healthy people enjoying themselves: attractive, self-confident women and self-assured, independent men.

A Step in the Right Direction

These billboards want you to believe that smoking makes people happier, more popular, and more self-confident. Did smoking make *you* happier, more popular, and more self-confident? You have decided that you would be happier, more popular, and more self-confident if you quit smoking—and you have quit. But the tobacco companies want you back as a customer, and they have placed billboard ads where you will see them, hoping to attract you to their message. What can you do to resist their temptations?

A Suggestion

Design a billboard of your own that tells the truth about smoking. Tape it to the dashboard of your car, and whenever you see a tobacco company billboard, look at yours too.

Meals Can Be Relapse Triggers

Eating a meal can be a relapse trigger. Some smokers associate the end of a meal with having a cigarette. Certain kinds of food (Italian or Mexican, for example) may be especially strong stimulants to smoke. Some smokers smoke only during their lunch hour; therefore, these people may associate lunch with smoking. Other people smoke more at home in the evening, so supper may be a stronger trigger for them.

A Step in the Right Direction

Did you often smoke with meals? Which meals of the day make you want to smoke? Which kinds of food make you want to smoke? These triggers to relapse may remain with you for months. When you sit in the nonsmoking side of a restaurant, do you feel out of place? Do you glance over at the smoking section and wish you were over there? When you are with a group of people at a meal, do you want to smoke?

A Suggestion

If you have a strong desire to smoke after a meal, tell your companions at the start of the meal that you know you are going to want a cigarette (this acknowledges your feelings) but that you have decided not to smoke (this shows your determination). Most likely you will receive support and encouragement.

Share Your Story with Someone

Relapses are common in all addictions, including nicotine and tobacco dependence. The relapse rate of recovering smokers is similar to the relapse rates of recovering alcoholics. When recovering alcoholics relapse, they usually feel ashamed, angry, and depressed; when recovering smokers relapse, they usually experience these same feelings. Trying to comfort relapsed smokers does little good. A better strategy is to encourage them to take action to quit again instead of spending time feeling sorry for themselves. The sooner they get started working on their recovery, the easier it will be. If they continue smoking for more than a few days, getting clean and free again will be much harder. Many never make another serious attempt to quit smoking.

A Step in the Right Direction

Do you know one or more recovering smokers who have relapsed? What can you do to help?

A Suggestion

Share with them your knowledge that most smokers make several serious attempts at quitting before they are successful—use your own story as an illustration. Offer to help them identify their relapse triggers. This will help you, too, because as you share your knowledge, you will be reminding *yourself* how to avoid a relapse.

Do You Smoke after Sex?

Some smokers automatically reach for a cigarette after having sex. If one partner still smokes, that person may reach for a cigarette after having sex; the recovering partner may automatically reach for one, too, forgetting for the moment that he or she no longer smokes. In relationships where neither person smokes, recovering smokers may still feel so uncomfortable without a cigarette that the pleasure of the moment is destroyed. They feel agitated and tense instead of satisfied and relaxed, and they may blame their partners when their discomfort is really due to their nicotine and tobacco dependence.

A Step in the Right Direction

Did you usually smoke after having sex? How about your partner? Since you quit smoking, have you reached for a cigarette after having sex, forgetting momentarily that you no longer smoke? If so, and if there were cigarettes on the nightstand, you might have taken one and smoked it. If that ever happens, the chances are that you would start smoking again. What can you do to eliminate the relapse trigger of smoking after having sex?

A Suggestion

Tell your partner about the progress you have made in recovery. Your chances of staying clean and free will improve dramatically when your partner joins you in working on recovery.

Should You Quit Smoking to Save Money?

One of the most common reasons smokers give for deciding to quit smoking is to save money. This reason is *serious* enough for them to quit, but it may not be *personal* enough for them to recover.

A Step in the Right Direction

In order to recover—not just quit smoking—you must make your reasons more personal.

A Suggestion

Respond to the following questions in your journal.

- Calculate how much money you used to spend buying cigarettes for one year. This is the money you gave the tobacco companies.
- Add the amount you spent on the extra dry cleaning and house cleaning you needed to do because of smoke pollution; then add the cost of property damage and lost time from work due to illnesses caused by smoking. This total represents how much money your smoking has cost you.

What Happened to Bill Wilson and Dr. Bob Smith?

Bill Wilson was an alcoholic. He tried to quit drinking in a dozen different ways, but in the 1930s, when he was a young man, little was known about treating alcoholism. One day, he had an idea: Perhaps he could quit drinking by accepting his addiction (instead of fighting it) and by helping other people stay sober (instead of just focusing on himself). Then Bill met Dr. Bob Smith, another alcoholic, and the two of them began helping each other. This was the start of Alcoholics Anonymous. Millions of men and women have quit drinking and using drugs through AA, and neither Bill nor Dr. Bob ever drank again after they founded AA. However, neither succeeded in stopping smoking, and both of them died from diseases caused by their smoking—Bill W. died from emphysema in 1971 at the age of seventy-five, and Dr. Bob died from cancer in 1950 at the age of seventy-one. Today, 75 percent of alcoholics smoke, and more alcoholics die from diseases caused by tobacco than from diseases caused by alcohol.

A Step in the Right Direction

Bill W. and Dr. Bob remained in denial about their dependence on nicotine and tobacco until their deaths. How long were you in denial? What did it take for you to accept the truth about your smoking?

A Suggestion

Identify some reasons why you have been able to quit smoking when neither Bill W. nor Dr. Bob could.

Structuring Your Day

After many years, cigarettes become an integral part of a smoker's life. Not only do cigarettes help smokers get through the day, they help smokers organize their days. Examples of such cigarettes include: the first one in the morning, the one on the way to work, the coffee-break cigarette, the lunchtime cigarette, the one at the end of the work day, and the last one at night. As the years go by, cigarettes become part of the structure of smokers' lives; when they quit smoking, they have to find other ways of structuring their time.

A Step in the Right Direction

Which cigarettes helped you organize your day? Have you felt uncomfortable at some of the times when you used to smoke? What are you doing now instead of smoking at those times?

A Suggestion

Identify three or four specific times of the day when you almost always smoked a cigarette. Plan activities to do at those times each day. If you don't do something active at those times, your thoughts will turn to smoking, putting you at greater risk of relapse. To stay clean and free, you will need to learn new ways of structuring your day.

Environmental Tobacco Smoke Can Be Deadly

In addition to killing more than 400,000 American smokers every year, smoking annually kills more than 50,000 American nonsmokers. Here's how: Smokers inhale *mainstream smoke* directly from their cigarettes; when they exhale, they fill the air with *secondhand smoke* (smoke partially filtered through their lungs) which nonsmokers then breathe. Nonsmokers also breathe in *sidestream smoke* (smoke from the burning tip of a cigarette). Together, secondhand smoke and sidestream smoke are called *environmental tobacco smoke,* which contains enough toxic chemicals to cause lung cancer and heart disease in nonsmokers who breathe it. Among these chemicals are formaldehyde, benzene, cyanide, arsenic, cadmium, pyrethrins, nitrosamines, radioactive polonium-210, and carbon monoxide.

A Step in the Right Direction

When you were smoking, were you aware that cigarette smoke could put nonsmokers at risk of getting cancer and heart disease? Did nonsmokers ever complain to you that your smoking bothered them? What did you say and do at the time? Here's the good news: now that you no longer smoke, you are not putting yourself or others at risk.

A Suggestion

Decide now how you will handle smokers whose cigarette smoke irritates you. How can you use your own experience as a smoker in a positive way?

Be Aware of Your Craving Triggers

Being in certain places or situations can make a recovering smoker want a cigarette. Here are some common trigger situations:

- Passing a certain landmark on the way to work
- Eating or drinking in a particular restaurant or bar
- Sitting in the departure area at the airport
- Waiting in line
- Being in an unfamiliar city
- Going to a party
- Sitting in a meeting
- Being stuck in traffic
- Getting cut off on the freeway

A Step in the Right Direction

Which of these situations have you experienced since you quit smoking? Did you think about smoking? What did you do to avoid smoking? What other places or situations can you think of that might be craving triggers for you?

A Suggestion

Make a list in your journal of half a dozen places where you still want to smoke.

One Day at a Time

Some smokers get into a smoking cessation program eagerly, but get bored after a while and start smoking again. Others stay enthusiastic as long as they have to struggle with their compulsion to smoke; when things get easier, they lose interest in working a recovery program and relapse unexpectedly. Still others set a short-term goal for staying clean, and when they reach that day, they go back to smoking.

A Step in the Right Direction

You have many opportunities to relapse every day. Which ones have been a threat to your recovery?

- Have you lost interest in your recovery?
- Have there been days when you felt like giving up?
- Does staying clean and free no longer seem like a challenge?
- Have you already achieved your goals?

When recovering smokers become apathetic or bored with their recovery program, relapse becomes possible.

A Suggestion

Make your recovery program part of your daily routine, like putting on your shoes. Select a time and a place for working on your recovery every day, and make it a part of your life.

A New Life

So many things change after a smoker gets into recovery. Recovering smokers develop new friends, pick up hobbies, and change their TV viewing and eating routines. They often discover that after a few months living clean and free, they are even waking up and going to sleep in a new pattern. They react to stress differently, handle strong emotions differently, and deal with other smokers differently. In short, every aspect of their lives has changed. Some recovering smokers are not prepared for these profound changes and cannot handle them; many of these people return to their old routines—and return to smoking.

A Step in the Right Direction

Do you miss some of your old routines? Have some of the changes been hard to get used to? Many recovering smokers resist changing their old routines, and this sets them up for relapse. Which of your routines have changed? Which old friends do you no longer see? How are you spending your time differently since you quit smoking?

A Suggestion

In your journal, list some of the changes you have become aware of. Most recovering smokers also discover that they have an extra hour or two each day—the time they used to spend smoking. How are you spending your extra time?

Who Are You, Really?

After years of smoking, cigarettes become part of a smoker's identity. A person who smokes Marlboro cigarettes proudly identifies himself or herself as a "Marlboro smoker." A man who smokes Marlboros would feel foolish and uncomfortable smoking a Virginia Slims cigarette—even though the Philip Morris Company makes both brands and there is very little difference in the tobacco, the additives, or the level of toxic chemicals in the cigarettes. A smoker's choice of brands has more to do with image and identity than anything else. Thus, when a smoker quits smoking, he or she must define a new identity.

A Step in the Right Direction

What was your regular brand of cigarettes at the time you quit smoking? What other brands did you favor during your years as a smoker? Why did you settle on those brands?

A Suggestion

Identify the image that people have of a person who smokes your old brands of cigarettes. Is that the kind of person you really were? Being a smoker was once a part of your image—now, that has changed. Who are you now? Who do you intend to become? Try this exercise: Using a fresh page in your journal, write "I am . . ." twenty times down the left side of the page. Now complete each sentence differently. By the end of the page, you will have a better idea of who you really are.

Choosing Life

In the King James Version of the Bible, Deuteronomy 30:19, it is written: "I have set before you life and death, blessings and curses. Now choose life, so that you and your children may live."

A Step in the Right Direction

The Bible tells us to choose life over death. Quitting smoking is an example of choosing life. Cigarettes represent death; they are instruments of death, sold by tobacco companies to eager smokers who are controlled by their addiction. Why did you choose death over life for so long?

A Suggestion

In your journal describe how quitting smoking is a victory of life over death and of blessings over curses. If it helps you, you can pair your thoughts in this way:

- My smoking gave me high blood pressure and bronchitis.
  - Now that I have quit smoking, my health has improved.

- My smoking put me at risk of getting cancer.
  - By quitting smoking, I will add five to fifteen years to my life.

- My family had given up hope that I would ever quit smoking.
  - Everyone in my family is proud of me for quitting smoking.

Smoking Was Part of Many Behaviors

People develop patterns of behavior in their daily activities, such as the way they comb their hair, the way they shave or put on makeup, and how they answer the phone. Doing things the same way helps people feel more secure and in control of their lives. Since smokers usually smoke cigarettes from the first thing in the morning to the last thing at night (and nearly every hour in between), cigarettes become part of many of these repetitive patterns.

A Step in the Right Direction

What were some of the things you used to do that included smoking a cigarette? What are you doing in these situations now instead of smoking?

A Suggestion

Choose one such situation and see how smoking was a part of it by writing down, step by step, what your actions were. Answering the telephone is an example:

- You heard the telephone ring and you went to the phone.
- You picked up the receiver while you took out a package of cigarettes.
- You pulled a cigarette out of the pack while you said "Hello."
- You lit the cigarette while the other person answered.
- You inhaled deeply before answering.

What role did cigarettes play in the situation you selected?

Image Is Nothing

Cigarette advertisements show adults having fun together; this influences children—who want to feel older and more mature—to start smoking. The same ads influence adults—who want to be youthful, vigorous, and popular—to continue smoking. Different advertisements appeal to different people. The tobacco companies know this and carefully craft an image for each of their brands:

- Marlboros are for tough, independent people
- Virginia Slims are for self-reliant women
- Camels are for fun-loving young adults
- Newports are for active people
- Carltons are for people who are concerned about their health

The tobacco companies create new brands every year, hoping that one will become popular.

A Step in the Right Direction

Which new brands have you noticed? What image did the tobacco companies promote for them? Now that you are no longer smoking, can you see how ridiculous their promotions are?

A Suggestion

Design a new brand of cigarettes for a fictitious group that doesn't have one yet. Now design an advertising campaign to promote your new brand. How does it feel to be a tobacco advertising executive?

Do You Want to Smoke When You Are with Certain People?

Being with certain people can make a recovering smoker want a cigarette. These people trigger memories and strong emotions in the recovering smoker.

A Step in the Right Direction

Did you use cigarettes to deal with strong emotions? If so, you may have an overwhelming desire to smoke when you are with certain people. It's not their fault—the feelings are yours, not theirs. But unless you deal with your feelings, you will not stay clean and free for long.

A Suggestion

Think of people who make you feel each of the following emotions; then identify why you feel that way when you are with them.

- Angry
- Afraid
- Irritated
- Youthful
- Playful
- Needed
- Inadequate

- Disappointed
- Resentful
- Frustrated
- Happy
- Desirable
- Sexually attracted
- Disrespected

Did You Rely on Cigarettes?

Smokers learn to trust their cigarettes, often more than they trust their human friends. Friends can be fickle and unreliable, but cigarettes are consistent. Friends have good days and bad ones, but every day is the same to a cigarette. Even long-time friends can do unpredictable things and may put their own needs first—but not cigarettes. They are always predictable, giving all and asking nothing. Whenever a smoker turns to a cigarette for help—to relax, to stay alert, to pass the time, or to deal with stress—the cigarette delivers.

A Step in the Right Direction

Did you rely on cigarettes to relax, to stay alert, to pass the time, or to deal with stress? When you turned to cigarettes, did they deliver as expected? Cigarettes were once your companion, right there when you needed them. Now that you are no longer smoking, how have you dealt with these situations?

A Suggestion

Identify a specific example of when you relied on cigarettes to relax, to stay alert, to pass the time, and to deal with stress. In your journal, describe each event and how cigarettes helped you. Following each description, make some notes on how you have been coping with each situation as a nonsmoker. Understanding how you once relied on cigarettes will help you stay clean and free.

End Your Relationship with Tobacco

Ending a relationship is difficult and stressful. Every smoker has a special and unique relationship with tobacco. While some smokers can quit smoking with just information and advice, those that cannot must examine their relationship with tobacco more closely. Many recovering smokers have developed a closer and more intimate relationship with tobacco than they ever did with people; ending such an intense relationship is not easy.

A Step in the Right Direction

How long did you have a relationship with tobacco? How did you feel about ending it? When lovers break up, they sometimes say, "We'll still be friends"; everyone knows that rarely works. Have you secretly hoped that you and tobacco could remain "in touch," and that one day you might get back together again? If so, you are leaving yourself at a high risk of relapse. To stay clean and free, you must end your relationship with tobacco completely and forever.

A Suggestion

Writing a "Good-bye" letter to tobacco is one way of finalizing this divorce. If you have already written one, pull it out, read it over, and add things that you have learned over the last month. If you have not written one, start today. Start with "Good-bye Tobacco," and tell tobacco why you have left it behind.

Smokers Treat Their Cigarettes Like a Special Friend

Smokers treat their cigarettes like a special friend. They keep them in a certain place, call them by name, and give them great respect. They share good times and troubled times with their cigarettes. When they are on a limited budget or short of cash, they often buy cigarettes before they buy food. People go for days or weeks without seeing or thinking about some of their friends, but smokers never go for more than a few hours without sharing a few minutes with their cigarettes. When smokers are away from their cigarettes, they think about them and anticipate getting together again. As soon as they can, they rush back to embrace their cigarettes.

A Step in the Right Direction

When you were still smoking, did you treat your cigarettes like a special friend?

A Suggestion

Make a list of some of the good times you shared with your cigarettes. How did your cigarettes make the good times better? Then make a list of some of the bad times you shared with your cigarettes. How did your cigarettes help you deal with the bad times? Some smokers make tremendous sacrifices in order to keep smoking. What sacrifices did you make? In what other ways did you treat your cigarettes like a special friend?

Make Your Car a Clean and Free Place

Driving a car can be a relapse trigger. Cars are private havens in public places; what goes on in cars always seems confidential. People who never smoke in their houses or offices may smoke constantly while driving their cars. Many smokers automatically light a cigarette when they get behind the wheel, even before they start the car. Some smokers light up a cigarette whenever the traffic slows down, particularly if they are in a hurry to get somewhere. When these people quit smoking, every ride in a car represents a relapse trigger for them.

A Step in the Right Direction

When you were smoking, did you smoke in your car? Which situations associated with driving a car especially made you want to smoke (such as being caught in traffic, being cut off by someone, being late, or having your car break down)? Since you quit smoking, have you been tempted to smoke while driving? What can you do to minimize your risk of relapse when driving a car?

A Suggestion

Make your car a special place for staying clean and free. Vacuum the carpet, the seats, and all the little crevices where cigarette ashes might be hiding. Scrub out the ashtrays. Wash down the windows, the dashboard, and the upholstery. This will reduce your interest in smoking in your car.

Being a Willing Listener

Relapses are common in all addictions, including nicotine and tobacco dependence. Relapsed smokers often feel isolated and rejected, full of self-blame and guilt. These feelings push them further into isolation, which delays their recovery. They rarely seek help when they want it the most because they are afraid they will be criticized and shamed. Since many have relapsed before (and suffered feelings of guilt and shame because of it), they expect others to treat them the same way again.

A Step in the Right Direction

Do you know one or more recovering smokers who have relapsed? Every day that relapsed smokers continue to smoke makes it that much harder for them to quit again. What could you do to help someone in this situation?

A Suggestion

Become a willing listener for someone in relapse. Relapsed smokers benefit from having someone listen to them without judging them, someone who acknowledges their feelings. You don't have to be a therapist to be of help—just a willing listener. Indicate your concern by paying attention to what they say; show you understand their feelings by not giving advice unless asked for it. Imagine if it were you who had relapsed; how would you want a willing listener to behave?

Dealing with Aggressive Smokers

Recovering smokers are often tempted to smoke when smokers offer them a cigarette. Some of these smokers may be more aggressive than expected, and the recovering smoker may accept a cigarette just to avoid a conflict.

A Step in the Right Direction

If you refuse the offer of a cigarette, saying, "I don't smoke anymore," your friends will support you. Most smokers will also think, *Yeah, I should probably quit too.* However, you may come across a few aggressive smokers who won't take no for an answer. They may even become threatening, saying something like, "Oh, so my cigarettes aren't good enough for you—is that it?" or "Well, look who's got religion!" Have you been in a situation like this? How will you respond when you are? Will you go ahead and accept a cigarette to avoid more conflict?

A Suggestion

Since logic and reason won't help you in this situation, try something completely unexpected. Start coughing and wheezing and say, "See why I quit? I'm so allergic to cigarette smoke, my lungs shut down completely when I smell it." Does this sound extreme to you? Don't reject this strategy out of hand—aggressive smokers are not easy to deal with, and you may need a surprise defense one day to stay clean and free. What other good responses have you thought of?

Identifying Personal Reasons to Quit

One of the most common reasons smokers give for deciding to quit smoking is that they feel hypocritical when they are smoking. This reason is *serious* enough for them to quit, but it may not be *personal* enough for them to recover.

A Step in the Right Direction

In order to recover—not just quit smoking—you must make your reasons more personal.

A Suggestion

Respond to the following questions in your journal.

- Did you ever promise to quit smoking, knowing that you never intended to fulfill the promise?
- When you were still smoking, did you ever tell a child not to smoke?
- Have you gone on a diet, eaten fresh vegetables and lots of fiber, eaten less cholesterol and fat, or started an exercise program—but continued to smoke?
- Did you ever tell someone that you had quit smoking, even though you fully intended to smoke again that same day?
- Did you ever say you had quit smoking, but what you had really done was to quit buying cigarettes and start "borrowing" cigarettes?

Setting Goals for the Future

Relapses are common in all addictions, including nicotine and tobacco dependence. When smokers succeed in quitting smoking, they set new, ambitious goals for themselves—goals like getting in shape, completing their education, finding a better job, and making plans for the future. They know they will be healthier and live longer, so they make plans to enjoy their new lease on life. If they relapse, they often feel so devastated that they abandon their goals.

A Step in the Right Direction

Do you know one or more recovering smokers who have relapsed? Did they lose hope in the future and faith in their abilities? What can you do to help?

A Suggestion

Help relapsed smokers focus on short-term goals immediately after a relapse, goals such as asking friends and family for support, setting a new Quit Day, cleaning out their ashtrays, and removing reminders about smoking. Success at short-term goals will give them confidence that they can quit again. Long-term goals, such as getting a new job, moving to a different city, or going back to school often seem overwhelming to a smoker who has recently relapsed, but short-term goals are more manageable. What other short-term goals can you think of?

Heal Your Lungs with Guided Imagery

Use guided imagery to heal your inflamed lungs.

A Step in the Right Direction

Guided imagery is a valuable strategy for relaxing your body while focusing the power of your mind. Here is a guided imagery exercise you can use; you will find others as you move through this book.

Plan to do this exercise for about five minutes. Sit in a comfortable chair or lie down, legs and arms uncrossed. Close your eyes, and breathe slowly and deeply. With each deep breath, imagine yourself becoming more and more relaxed. Focus on your breathing. Continue to breathe deeply, allowing all the concerns of the day to leave your mind as the air leaves your lungs. When your body is thoroughly relaxed, turn your attention to your lung passages, the trachea and the bronchi. Search through your lung passages for signs of infection. Look for collections of pus, pockets of slimy fungus, and stagnant pools of bacteria. Signal your lungs to cough up the infected mucus and spit it out. Get rid of the slime so your lungs are clean again. Continue to breathe deeply and relax. After about five minutes, open your eyes and notice how you feel.

A Suggestion

Use guided imagery every day to help your body and your mind heal.

Associations with Smoking Number 1

Smokers often associate smoking with something they do, such as shaving or putting on makeup, getting dressed, reading a book, watching TV, working in the yard, doing housework, fixing things, listening to music, having sex, eating a meal, and playing cards.

A Step in the Right Direction

Which activities did you associate with smoking? You are at risk for relapse whenever you do any of them now. You can avoid some of them, but not all—you still have to get dressed and eat food. What can you do to reduce your risk of relapse in these situations?

A Suggestion

Change your patterns of behavior to reduce the association with smoking. Try one of these alternatives today:

- Get dressed in a different room.
- Put your clothes on in a different order.
- Take a different route to work.
- Eat lunch with different people.
- Sit in a different place at the dinner table.
- Have sex in a different room than usual.

Changing your patterns of behavior can help you stay clean and free.

Associations with Smoking Number 2

Smokers often associate smoking with something they see. Here are some examples:

- The flare of a lighter and the billow of smoke as someone lights a cigarette
- People smoking and enjoying their cigarettes
- A pack of their old brand of cigarettes sitting on a table
- Billboards advertising cigarettes, especially their old brand
- Tobacco ads in magazines
- Cigarette butts on the ground or in an ashtray
- Cigarette smoke drifting upward in a restaurant

A Step in the Right Direction

What did you see today that made you think about smoking? What did you do about it? Unless you take action at times like these, the visual associations with smoking can put you at risk for relapse. Which situations still make you want to smoke? What can you do to reduce your risk of relapse in these situations?

A Suggestion

Carry a *Keep Quit* chip with you at all times, in your pocket or on a chain. When you see something that reminds you of smoking, immediately look at your chip. This action will replace the reminder of smoking with a reminder about staying clean and free.

Associations with Smoking Number 3

Smokers often associate smoking with something they hear. Here are some examples:

- The sound of a cigarette pack being opened
- The sound of the package's cellophane being crumpled
- The sound of a match or a lighter being struck
- The sound of a person sucking on a cigarette
- The sound of a person blowing out smoke

A Step in the Right Direction

What did you hear today that made you think about smoking? What did you do about it? Unless you take action at times like these, the sounds associated with smoking can put you at risk for relapse. Which sounds still make you want to smoke? What can you do to reduce your risk of relapse in these situations?

A Suggestion

Choose a song, a hymn, or some instrumental music that gives you a positive feeling and that reminds you about why you intend to stay clean and free. For example, you might choose Helen Reddy's "I Am Woman," Pete Seeger's "If I Had a Hammer," the hymn "Amazing Grace," or a passage from Beethoven's Seventh Symphony. When something you hear reminds you of smoking, immediately replace the sound of smoking with your recovery music.

Associations with Smoking Number 4

Smokers often associate smoking with something they smell, such as the smell of tobacco for sale at the grocery checkout counter, the smell of a cigarette being smoked, the smell of a match lighting a cigarette, the smell of pipe tobacco, and the smell of tobacco smoke on clothing. Many recovering smokers discover that when they smell something they once associated with smoking, they salivate, have abdominal cramps, get short of breath, feel their heart rates increase, and start sweating. They may even get a little dizzy.

A Step in the Right Direction

What did you smell today that made you think about smoking? What did you do about it? Unless you take action at times like these, the association of a particular smell with smoking can put you at risk for relapse. Which smoking-related situation would be the strongest reminder of smoking for you? What can you do to reduce your risk of relapse in that situation?

A Suggestion

When you smell something that reminds you of smoking, cough immediately. Coughing will interrupt the train of thought that can lead to relapse. As soon as possible, find some fresh air and fill your lungs with clean air instead of air polluted by tobacco smoke. What positive message can you give yourself when you do this?

Support Will Help You through Difficult Times

Every day, a recovering smoker receives thousands of invitations to relapse. The tobacco companies, active smokers, and the stresses of everyday life all encourage recovering smokers to return to their addiction.

A Step in the Right Direction

In order to stay clean and free, you must take action to improve the quality of your recovery every day. This is not an easy job. Have you been doing it alone, or have you accepted support from others? Support from others will help you through the more difficult times. How many invitations to relapse did you receive this week? Did you see some advertisements for cigarettes in magazines or on billboards? Did you see cigarettes for sale in a store or vending machine? Did someone offer you a cigarette? The day may come when you get tired of turning down these invitations to relapse and consider accepting one of them.

A Suggestion

Expand and strengthen your support network this week. What have you done to ensure that the support of your friends and family will be there when you need it most? Have you provided support to other recovering smokers whom you can call on when you need support? The more support you get, the better will be your chances of success.

Dealing with Unexpected Cravings

During smokers' first year of recovery, they may have times when they have especially strong cravings to smoke. In spite of doing everything right—staying away from reminders of smoking, dealing with stress, and staying healthy—cravings for a cigarette may appear without warning. No one knows why cravings appear like this; they are not due to nicotine withdrawal, and the specific trigger to smoke may not be apparent.

A Step in the Right Direction

You have already dealt with most of the obvious triggers to smoke: reminders of smoking, other people smoking, stress, and uncomfortable feelings. Have you also had cravings for a cigarette when none of these triggers were apparent? How can you protect yourself from an enemy you cannot see?

A Suggestion

Identify some activities that make smoking less desirable for you, such as brushing your teeth, drinking grapefruit juice, chewing fruit-flavored gum, reading the Bible, jogging, doing deep-breathing exercises, cleaning the house, baking cookies, kneading bread, or working on the car. Make a list of them for use in an emergency. If an unexpected craving to smoke suddenly intrudes into your day, drop what you're doing and do one of the things on your list. Keep track of the ones that have worked—you'll want to turn to them first.

Change Is Difficult

People resist making changes even when they know they would be better off if they did. The reasons people avoid change vary:

- Some people won't change because they expect to fail.
- Some people won't change because they are insecure about doing things in a new way.
- Some people won't change because it might mean they would have to admit that their old ways of doing things weren't right.

Quitting smoking is a major change in any smoker's life; most smokers think about quitting for years before they finally decide to quit. This is not surprising; smoking affects nearly everything a smoker does. It's no wonder that deciding to quit smoking takes a long time and that staying clean and free is so hard.

A Step in the Right Direction

When did you first seriously consider quitting smoking? How many times have you tried to quit?

A Suggestion

Identify just one problem that made it hard for you to quit in the past. What have you done to eliminate this barrier to success? If you do not eliminate this barrier, it will remain a relapse issue for you this time too. If you are serious about your recovery, you will deal with this issue today.

How to Help Others

Relapses are common in all addictions, including nicotine and tobacco dependence. Part of a successful relapse prevention program for recovering smokers includes helping others who are trying to quit smoking. Smokers who are trying to quit don't want advice from people who have never smoked—they want to hear from people who have successfully dealt with the same problems they are facing.

A Step in the Right Direction

How many times did you seriously attempt to quit smoking before you succeeded? Did you receive support, advice, or encouragement from someone who had previously quit? Giving help to others is one of the best ways to understand your own recovery.

A Suggestion

Search out one or two people who want to quit smoking but who are still reluctant, and do these four things:

- Compliment them for making the right decision.
- Tell them some of the personal reasons why you decided to quit smoking.
- Tell them how your life has improved since you quit smoking.
- Ask them about their personal reasons for wanting to quit smoking.

Helping someone else will help you understand your own recovery even better.

The Sights, Smells, and Sounds of Smoking

The senses of sight, smell, and hearing often provoke emotional reactions. The sight of the Statue of Liberty chokes up people who immigrated to America through Ellis Island, even if they arrived fifty years ago. The aroma of suntan lotion brings vacations at the beach immediately to mind. The recorded voice of Martin Luther King Jr. delivering his "I have a dream" speech still fills many people with hope for the future. These examples show how sights, smells, and sounds can affect emotions. Long after they have smoked their last cigarette, recovering smokers may still be attracted to the sights, smells, and sounds of smoking.

A Step in the Right Direction

Have you seen a lot of people smoking your old brand lately? Has the aroma of tobacco attracted you, drifting over from the smoking side of a restaurant or from across a parking lot? Has the sound of someone sucking on a cigarette caught your attention? How do you react to the sights, smells, and sounds of smoking?

A Suggestion

You can understand these reactions better through writing a "Good-bye" letter to tobacco. If you have already written one, pull it out, read it over, and add things that you have learned over the last month. If you have not written one, start today. Start with "Good-bye Tobacco," and tell tobacco why you have left it behind.

Recovery Is Your Top Priority

Some recovering smokers who relapse use the word "slip" to imply that their relapse was not really their fault, that it was an unavoidable accident. However, when relapsed smokers carefully review the events surrounding their relapses, they discover ways the relapse could have been prevented. Very often, they see how they did not give their recovery the attention it required. Staying clean and free requires working on recovery every day; when recovering smokers stop making recovery their first priority, they usually start smoking again.

A Step in the Right Direction

Recovering people in Alcoholics Anonymous sometimes say that "slip" stands for "Sobriety Loses Its Priority." Your recovery from nicotine and tobacco dependence is just like a recovering alcoholic's sobriety—unless you give it top priority, your chances of relapsing are high. Are you making your recovery your top priority or has it lost its priority in your life?

A Suggestion

Recall the last time you quit smoking for a period of time and then started smoking again. What did you place as a higher priority than your recovery? Make some notes in your journal about setting priorities for recovery.

Regain Control

For most recovering smokers, the first year after they quit smoking is the most difficult. They suffer from withdrawal symptoms (difficulty concentrating, anxiety, mood swings, irritability) and from frequent cravings for a cigarette. During the difficult first year, many recovering smokers say, "It's just not worth it" and return to smoking.

A Step in the Right Direction

The intense desire for a cigarette has defeated many recovering smokers during the first year after quitting. Has it defeated you in the past? You may have had moments when the desire to smoke seemed absolutely overwhelming. There may have been days when you thought, "I just can't take any more of this. Maybe I'll just go back to smoking." These were moments when your addiction was trying to take back control of your thoughts and feelings.

A Suggestion

The next time the desire to smoke comes over you, rate your desire for a cigarette on a scale of one to ten (ten is the strongest; one is the weakest). Make a decision to wait just ten minutes before giving in and smoking; then rate your desire for a cigarette again. Chances are, the rating will be lower. If it is, you have proven that you *can* regain control of your thoughts and feelings by making a serious effort. Will you make that effort today?

Stress Can Trigger a Relapse

Recovering smokers must learn to identify high-risk situations in their everyday lives. Here are a few of them:

- Sitting around a table with friends who are smoking at a coffee break
- Drinking in a smoky bar in an unfamiliar city
- Waiting for a delayed flight in an airport departure lounge
- Getting stuck in traffic
- Staying up late at night with friends
- Visiting a sick friend or relative

A Step in the Right Direction

Being in stressful situations can increase your risk of relapse. Which everyday situations still represent high-risk threats to you? Since you quit smoking, which stressful situations have you learned to avoid?

A Suggestion

In your journal, list a few of the situations you have been successful at avoiding. How were you successful at avoiding them? Which stressful situations have you been unable to avoid? List a few of these in your journal as well, pairing each one with a stressful situation you have learned to avoid. What worked for the situations in the first column that you could apply to the situations in the second column?

Denial Precedes a Relapse

Over ten or twenty or more years of smoking, smokers eventually learn to ignore the minor day-to-day inconveniences of smoking, such as bad breath, smelly clothes, and scars burned into the furniture. This is a form of denial, the unconscious resistance to accepting the truth. They also develop deep denial about the serious long-term consequences of smoking, such as cancer, heart disease, emphysema, and stroke. Denial prevents smokers from dealing with reality: the reality that they have become completely dependent on nicotine and tobacco and that they are in danger of experiencing serious consequences from their smoking. Denial keeps them insulated from the truth and prevents them from deciding to quit.

A Step in the Right Direction

When you were smoking, did you ignore its day-to-day inconveniences? Did you also develop deep denial about the potential long-term consequences of your smoking? Most recovering smokers still hold on to a few shreds of denial. For example, they may continue to defend the irresponsible marketing practices of the tobacco companies or hesitate to ask a smoker to stop smoking in a nonsmoking area.

A Suggestion

List some examples in your journal of the denial that once controlled you. Are you still hanging on to a bit of denial?

Is Fatigue a Good Enough Reason to Quit?

One of the most common reasons smokers give for deciding to quit smoking is that they feel tired all the time. They usually know that smoking damages their lungs and their hearts, but what they notice is how fatigued they feel. This reason is *serious* enough for them to quit, but it may not be *personal* enough for them to recover.

A Step in the Right Direction

In order to recover—not just quit smoking—you must make your reasons more personal.

A Suggestion

Respond to the following questions in your journal.

- Were you frequently fatigued when you were smoking?
- How has your energy level improved since you quit smoking?
- What are you doing with your extra energy? Are you exercising more? (You will probably gain weight unless you do.)
- When you were smoking, did you blame your poor health on some other condition, when the problem was really your smoking?
- Now that you are clean and free, are you taking care of your body in other ways?
- What will you achieve as a nonsmoker that you could not have done as a smoker?

Avoid the Designated Smoking Area

So many public places no longer permit smoking that most smokers have to step outside to smoke. When they want to smoke, they have to leave the building; they get used to reaching for a cigarette as they walk through the door and lighting one when they get to their favorite smoking spot. After doing this hundreds of times, they associate stepping outside with smoking a cigarette. After they quit smoking, they may automatically reach for a cigarette when leaving a building, and they may crave a cigarette whenever they pass their old smoking spot. If they see an old smoking buddy there, they may automatically ask for a cigarette—and they may start smoking again.

A Step in the Right Direction

Did you regularly step outside to smoke? Did you have a particular place where you (and others) went to smoke? Merely being in that spot could start a chain reaction that leads to smoking. Do you still long to smoke when you walk outside? What can you do to eliminate stepping outside as a relapse trigger?

A Suggestion

Draw a little sign that says "Oxygen in use—thank you for not smoking" on the back of a business card and keep it in your wallet or purse. Each time you step outside for the next week, pull out your sign to remind yourself of your commitment to staying clean and free.

Making Changes

Many recovering smokers report that smoking was their greatest pleasure and that they have never found anything to replace it. Smoking perked them up when they were tired, gave them something to do with their hands when they were bored, and calmed them down when they were nervous. They used cigarettes to help them deal with tense situations and to help them fit in with their friends. Recovering smokers like these are in constant danger of relapse because they will never find anything that will do all those things as well as cigarettes once did. Unless they learn an entirely new way of living, a day will come when they are tired, or bored, or tense, or feeling left out, and they will start smoking again.

A Step in the Right Direction

Was smoking one of your greatest pleasures? Have you searched for a replacement (but failed to find one)? You will never find a perfect replacement for smoking, because cigarettes combine nicotine, smoke, image, and satisfying things to do in a unique package that nothing can duplicate. You have decided that you no longer want to be a smoker. What kind of person have you decided to be instead?

A Suggestion

Write a short list of the aspects about your character that you would like to change. What is still preventing you from making those changes?

The Smell of a Cigarette

For recovering smokers, the feel, sight, and smell of cigarettes are powerful relapse triggers. It's not so difficult to avoid touching cigarettes and packs of cigarettes, but it is impossible to avoid seeing and smelling cigarettes on a daily basis. As long as smokers continue to smoke in public places, the sights and smells of smoking will remain a constant relapse trigger for recovering smokers.

A Step in the Right Direction

You can reduce your contact with many relapse triggers and eliminate many more, but you will still see people smoking and you will still smell cigarette smoke every day. What can you do about it?

A Suggestion

Develop some motivational messages to use whenever you see someone smoking or whenever you smell cigarette smoke. Good motivational messages are short, crisp, and direct; they carry both emotional impact and information. Here are some examples:

- When you see someone smoking, tell yourself, "Cigarettes don't control me now."
- When you see your brand of cigarettes, tell yourself, "Ancient history."
- When you smell cigarette smoke, tell yourself, "I smell poison gas."

Create your own motivational messages and record them in your journal.

Accepting Responsibility

Relapses are common in all addictions, including nicotine and tobacco dependence. When people relapse after quitting, they may blame other people or events beyond their control. This may make them feel a little better about themselves for a while, but it does not help them achieve their ultimate goal—quitting smoking forever. Blaming others for a relapse usually results in another relapse; only by accepting responsibility for all their actions can recovering smokers understand the truth about their nicotine and tobacco dependence.

A Step in the Right Direction

Do you know one or more recovering smokers who have relapsed? A relapse can be a devastating experience or it can be a motivator. Many relapsed smokers view themselves as failures and give up; most of them will smoke until they die. Others pick themselves up and use their relapse to better understand their nicotine and tobacco dependence. They accept personal responsibility for their behavior and dedicate themselves to learning how to prevent another relapse. How can you help smokers who have relapsed?

A Suggestion

Tell them how you have learned to take responsibility for your own actions and how this has helped you stay clean and free. What have you learned about *yourself* through your recovery from nicotine and tobacco dependence?

Dependence on Nicotine and Tobacco
Controls Smokers

Smokers usually say that they smoke when they want to, but actually they smoke when their addiction demands it. This is an example of *denial:* the inability of smokers to recognize and accept the truth about their smoking. It's too painful to accept that their thoughts and behavior are being controlled by cigarettes, so they give other reasons for smoking. This is not a conscious choice. Denial is an unconscious process; smokers in denial actually believe the excuses they make. Therefore, arguing with them or punishing them does not improve their chances of recovery—and it may drive them deeper into denial.

A Step in the Right Direction

When you were smoking, how deep was your denial? How can understanding denial help you stay clean and free?

A Suggestion

Recall when you were a smoker in denial. Did your dependence on nicotine and tobacco . . .

- Control how you spent your time and your money?
- Dictate with whom you spent time?
- Decide with whom you would have a serious relationship?
- Control how long you continued a conversation?

Make some notes in your journal about your own experiences with denial.

Use Your Imagination to Stay Clean and Free

Seeing others smoking can be a relapse trigger for a recovering smoker—*especially* if they are smoking a familiar brand, and especially if they are really enjoying their cigarette. At such a moment, a recovering smoker may wonder, "Maybe I could smoke *just one.*" Research shows that if a recovering smoker takes even a single puff off a cigarette, his or her chances of being clean and free six months later drop to 5 percent.

A Step in the Right Direction

When you see someone smoking, what is the first thought that pops into your head? Do you think positively: "I'm really glad I quit smoking"? Do you take an arrogant attitude: "So sad—I guess he can't quit"? Do you imagine yourself with a cigarette in your hand: "That looks pretty good . . . wish I had one"? Imagining yourself smoking can open the door to relapse. However, if you can imagine yourself smoking, you can also imagine yourself *not smoking.*

A Suggestion

When you see people smoking and you want a cigarette too, imagine the smoke spreading poison through their bodies and eating away at their lungs, the way it once did to you. Then imagine your own lungs, clean and free of toxic smoke. Which vision do you prefer?

Stay Focused

Football players talk to each other about football. Doctors talk to each other about medicine. Smokers talk to each other about smoking. These days, public opinion is against smoking in public, so smokers often feel isolated and threatened. When they talk about smoking, it's not about quitting—it's about how much they like smoking and about how unfair the world has been to smokers.

A Step in the Right Direction

Many of your old friends were smokers and some still are. When you are with them, the conversation may turn to smoking. Warning: These conversations may be hazardous to your health! They can wear down your resistance and put you at risk for relapse. How can you avoid putting yourself at risk of relapse because of such a conversation?

A Suggestion

Refocus the conversation from *smoking* to *recovery from smoking*. When you hear "Remember the time when . . . ," you can predict that what follows will be a reminiscence about the pleasures of smoking. Refocus the conversation by saying, "You know, since I quit smoking. . . ." If your friends persist in wanting to glorify smoking, it is time to walk away from the conversation.

Handling Stress, Not Cigarettes

Some smokers really look forward to the handling aspects of smoking—opening a pack, holding a cigarette, feeling it, lighting it, tapping off its ash, and crushing it out. Handling a cigarette reduces their anxiety and helps them cope with stress. After they quit smoking, they no longer have cigarettes to handle and they get more anxious.

A Step in the Right Direction

Did you enjoy the handling aspects of smoking? What were some of the special little things you did with a cigarette? Do you miss having a cigarette to hold and handle? If you started smoking as a teenager, you may not have developed enough other effective coping skills, and this may be a significant relapse issue for you.

A Suggestion

In time, you will learn new and more effective ways of dealing with stressful situations, but for now, use another handling activity to help you deal with stress. The first thing to try is a *Keep Quit* chip; you might also try a plastic stirstick, a paper clip, a pencil, a soda straw, or a toothpick. Use your handling substitute all the time at first. As time goes on, you will find it less and less necessary because you are learning other ways to deal with situations that used to upset you. However, there is nothing wrong with continuing to use a handling replacement indefinitely if it helps you avoid a relapse.

Has Drinking Been a Problem?

The 1987 National Health Interview Survey interviewed 44,000 Americans about their smoking and their use of alcohol and other drugs. The results showed that 31 percent of men and 26.5 percent of women smoked; the highest rates were in the twenty-five- to forty-four-year-old age group. Of those who smoked, 11 percent were heavy beer drinkers; only 3 percent of people who had never smoked were heavy beer drinkers. Research conducted by the University of Texas Medical School at Houston showed that 73 percent of alcoholics entering treatment were also dependent on nicotine and tobacco.

A Step in the Right Direction

Have you noticed that drinking and smoking tend to go together? When you were smoking, did you smoke more when you were drinking alcohol? Now that you are no longer smoking, does your desire to smoke increase when you drink alcohol or when you are around people who are drinking alcohol?

A Suggestion

Take a close look at your own use of alcohol. After quitting smoking, many recovering smokers realize that their alcohol use is a problem; they never noticed the problem until they quit smoking. Could your drinking be a problem? (If this suggestion upsets you, you might want to take an even closer look at this question.)

Learn from Your Successes

Stress is a part of everyday life, and smokers learn to rely on cigarettes to give them a chemical lift in moments of stress. Soon, this becomes an automatic response: whenever smokers hear bad news, they reach for a cigarette. The nicotine dulls their emotional pain the same way a narcotic dulls physical pain. When the nicotine wears off, the pain is still there, so they want—they need—another cigarette; this cycle keeps them addicted. Recovering smokers must develop new coping skills to deal with stress.

A Step in the Right Direction

Did you use cigarettes to help you deal with emotional stress and emotional pain? How well did it work for you? Now, you no longer have cigarettes to rely on in moments of stress. How have you been dealing with stress since you quit smoking?

A Suggestion

Identify three stressful events that occurred in your life during the last week. Did you think about smoking in these situations? Would you have turned to a cigarette in these situations when you were still smoking? Each time you deal with a stressful event and do not smoke you strengthen your recovery. What did you learn about yourself and your recovery from the three events you named? What coping skills did you rely on? When will you be able to use your skills again next week?

What Happened to Victor Crawford?

Victor Crawford was an attorney who once served in the legislature in the state of Maryland. Later, he worked as a lobbyist in the Maryland legislature for the Tobacco Institute; his job was to defeat bills the tobacco companies didn't like. One of them was a bill that would ban smoking in restaurants in Maryland. On the *60 Minutes* television show, Crawford described how he lied to the legislators, how he concocted fake scientific evidence, and how he commissioned bogus public opinion polls—all on the instructions of his employer, the Tobacco Institute. They paid Crawford plenty to work for them, but he also did the job because he was a confirmed smoker and loved to smoke. Then a few years ago, he developed a highly malignant cancer, and the cancer spread throughout his body. That's when he decide to quit smoking. Before he passed away recently, he gave talks about the dangers of smoking. He also lobbied in the legislature *against* smoking, and he helped pass a tough new law in Maryland to ensure clean air in public buildings.

A Step in the Right Direction

Have you had a change of opinion about smoking, smokers, and the tobacco industry?

A Suggestion

Tell your story to others, just like Victor Crawford did. Your story of success can make a real difference.

Pleasurable and Controlling Aspects of Smoking

In 1622, Sir Francis Bacon wrote in his book *Historia Vital et Mortis:* "The use of tobacco conquers men with a certain secret pleasure so that those who have once become accustomed thereto can hardly be restrained therefrom."

A Step in the Right Direction

What pleasures did you get from tobacco? When did you first become "accustomed" to smoking? When did you discover that you could not "restrain" yourself from daily smoking? Have you dealt with both the pleasurable and the addictive aspects of tobacco?

A Suggestion

Make a list of the pleasures you got from smoking. Pair each item with an example of how smoking controlled your thoughts, feelings, and behavior. Here are some examples:

- Smoking relaxed me when I was tense and perked me up when I was drowsy.

  - I came to rely on smoking to calm me down and keep me alert.

- Smoking helped me concentrate when I needed to think clearly.

  - Since I used cigarettes to stay alert, I didn't always bother to get enough sleep.

- Smoking made me feel more mature and a part of the crowd when I was young.

  - I still felt awkward, lonely, and inadequate—I just didn't show it.

Set Recovery as Your Goal

Recovery from smoking has three phases: Stop, Quit, and Recover. *Stop* is what smokers do when they walk into a non-smoking building; they don't smoke, but they fully intend to smoke again as soon as they walk out the door. *Quit* means that they have stopped smoking and do not intend to smoke again—although many do. *Recover* means that they have accepted their dependence on nicotine and tobacco, they no longer need to rely on a chemical to deal with their feelings, and they have decided that smoking again is simply not one of their options. Recovering smokers do something positive every day to improve the quality of their recovery. These are the people with the best chance of staying clean and free.

A Step in the Right Direction

What is your goal: to stop, to quit, or to recover? You have *stopped* smoking thousands of times, but when did you first *quit* smoking? How is this time different from the other times? Have you set *recovery* as your goal this time? Why?

A Suggestion

This is a good question to discuss in your "Good-bye" letter to tobacco. If you have already written one , pull it out, read it over, and add things that you have learned over the last few months. If you have not written one, start today. Start with "Good-bye Tobacco," and tell tobacco why you have left it behind.

Cigarettes Became Your Best Friend

Smokers develop a special relationship with their cigarettes. After many years of smoking, smokers adopt cigarettes as their best friend. Smokers discover that they can trust their cigarettes more than they can trust people. Unlike human friends, cigarettes are reliable and consistent, and are always willing to spend time with their smoker. In return, smokers become intensely loyal to their best friend, cigarettes. They keep them close, defend them, and buy them gifts (like fancy cases and T-shirts decorated with their name). They even insist on having a special place in restaurants where they can be together.

A Step in the Right Direction

Did cigarettes become your best friend? If so, when did this happen?

A Suggestion

Recall when you first trusted cigarettes more than you trusted people. This is when cigarettes became your best friend, the one you really relied on. Describe in your journal what your close friendship with cigarettes meant to you. Give some examples of the ways you trusted your cigarettes with your feelings. How did you turn to cigarettes for support and friendship? You and your cigarettes became best friends, but as the years passed, that relationship deepened even further. Understanding your relationship with cigarettes and how it changed over the years will help you stay clean and free.

Keeping a Positive Outlook on the Future

Relapses are common in all addictions, including nicotine and tobacco dependence. Quitting smoking gives people hope for the future; relapses can destroy that hope. Hope is what gives people the energy they need to change their self-destructive and self-defeating behaviors. When they start smoking again, many relapsed smokers lose hope in the future and lose faith in themselves. Relapsed smokers often doubt that they will ever be able to stay clean and free, and put off setting a new Quit Date. But the longer they continue to smoke, the harder it is for them to quit again.

A Step in the Right Direction

Have you had days when you lost faith in yourself or doubted that you would be able to quit smoking? Since you quit smoking, have you been "this" close to relapse? Something kept you going, because you're clean and free today. Do you know one or more recovering smokers who have relapsed? Did they lose faith in themselves? What can you do to help?

A Suggestion

Share with them how quitting smoking has improved your outlook on the future. Helping those who have relapsed regain hope for the future may be the most important thing you can do for them. Only when they have hope will they make another effort to quit smoking. Let your positive attitude rub off on them.

Smoking Causes Arteriosclerosis

Smoking leads to the deaths of over 400,000 Americans every year, according to the surgeon general. Components of the "tar" in cigarette smoke cause the body to deposit fatty material and cholesterol inside a smoker's arteries—a process called "arteriosclerosis" or "hardening of the arteries." These deposits clog up the arteries throughout the body; blockage in the arteries in the brain leads to strokes, blockage in the arteries feeding the heart leads to heart attacks, and blockage in the aorta (the body's largest artery) can cause the aorta to rupture.

A Step in the Right Direction

Have you been concerned about arteriosclerosis? Do you have a family history of high cholesterol, high blood pressure, or diabetes? A family history of one of those problems indicates that you are already at higher risk of arteriosclerosis than other people. Here's the good news: now that you have quit smoking, your blood vessels have already started to heal. Research shows that reducing the fat and cholesterol in your diet and exercising regularly also help.

A Suggestion

Assess your overall health. Now that you have quit smoking, look at some of your other behaviors. Which ones may be unhealthy? Are you willing to change some things in your life so you can live longer?

Quitting Smoking to Live Longer

A lifetime of smoking takes five to fifteen years off a smoker's life; many smokers quit smoking in order to live longer. This reason is certainly *serious* enough for them to quit, but it may not be *personal* enough for them to recover.

A Step in the Right Direction

You have known for years that smoking could shorten your life, but it wasn't enough of a reason to get you to quit. In order to recover—not just quit smoking—you must make your reasons more personal.

A Suggestion

Respond to the following questions in your journal.

- How will you spend the extra five to fifteen years you will live because you have quit smoking?
- What personal goals will you accomplish in that time?
- What places will you visit in those extra years of life?
- Whose lives do you want to be a part of in those extra years of life?
- What place in the world will you have a chance to visit because you will live longer as a nonsmoker?
- How can you use those extra years to reward yourself for staying clean and free?

Theories of Addiction Part 1

Scientists, psychologists, and physicians hold a variety of opinions to explain why people become addicted to alcohol, cocaine, nicotine, or any other drug. Over the next few days, we will look at some of the theories—twelve in all. Here are the first three:

- Addictions are genetic diseases, like muscular dystrophy. Addicts are born, not made. It's in their genes and they can't do anything about it.
- Addictions are environmental diseases, like skin cancer or lead poisoning. People become addicts because of exposure to the drug. No exposure, no addiction.
- Addictions are moral failings, like cheating. Addicts are bad people. People who smoke are morally weak.

A Step in the Right Direction

Do any of these theories of addiction explain your dependence on nicotine and tobacco? Do you have an emotional reaction to them?

A Suggestion

In your journal, describe ways in which each of these three theories explains something about your smoking history. Which one explains your dependence on nicotine and tobacco the best? Based on that theory of addiction, what do you have to do to stay clean and free?

Theories of Addiction Part 2

No one knows why people become addicted, but there are many theories. Yesterday, we looked at three of them. Here are three more:

- Addictions are learned behavior, like being late all the time. People can learn new behaviors to replace the old ones if they make the effort.
- Addictions are due to an enzyme deficiency, like lactose deficiency. People are either born without the correct enzyme levels or their enzyme levels become abnormal during their lives.
- Addictions are due to brain cell deterioration, like Alzheimer's disease. The brain cells of addicts no longer function normally.

A Step in the Right Direction

Do any of these theories of addiction explain your dependence on nicotine and tobacco? Do you have an emotional reaction to them?

A Suggestion

In your journal, describe ways in which each of these three theories explains something about your smoking history. Which one explains your dependence on nicotine and tobacco the best? Based on that theory of addiction, what do you have to do to stay clean and free?

Theories of Addiction Part 3

Medical scientists have struggled for years to understand why some people become addicted and others do not. Over the past two days, we have looked at six different theories of addiction. Here are three more:

- Addictions are personal choices, like going off a diet. People can stop if they want to. Anyone can stop smoking if they just want to badly enough.
- Addictions are symptoms of a psychiatric disorder, such as depression. Treat the underlying disorder and the addiction will disappear, because it is only a symptom.
- Addictions are part of a personality disorder, such as antisocial personality. Addicts use chemicals because their personality is flawed.

A Step in the Right Direction

Do any of these theories of addiction explain your dependence on nicotine and tobacco? Do you have an emotional reaction to them?

A Suggestion

In your journal, describe ways in which each of these three theories explains something about your smoking history. Which one explains your dependence on nicotine and tobacco the best? Based on that theory of addiction, what do you have to do to stay clean and free?

Theories of Addiction Part 4

There are many theories to explain why some people become addicted and others do not. Over the past three days, we have looked at nine such theories. Here are three more:

- Addictions are compulsions, like obsessive-compulsive disorder. They are due to a chemical imbalance in the brain that makes people do the same irrational things over and over again.
- Addictions are due to a chemical imbalance in the brain, like manic-depressive disorder. If chemical balance could be restored, the disorder would be cured.
- Addictions are diseases with no single cause, like diabetes mellitus. They can only be explained by a combination of genetic, developmental, and environmental factors.

A Step in the Right Direction

Do any of these theories of addiction explain your dependence on nicotine and tobacco?

A Suggestion

In your journal, describe ways in which each of these three theories explains something about your smoking history. Which of the twelve theories of addiction discussed over the past four days explains your dependence on nicotine and tobacco the best? Based on that theory of addiction, what do you have to do to stay clean and free?

Handling Stress without Smoking

Stress is a part of everyday life. Four typical causes of stress include:

- Conflicts with other people
- Concerns about families
- Fears about the future
- Bitterness about events from the past

Smokers use cigarettes to help them cope with stresses like these; after they quit smoking, they must learn new ways of dealing with stress. If they don't, they usually return to smoking.

A Step in the Right Direction

Have you learned some new strategies for dealing with stress? Has stress been a cause of relapse for you in the past? If so, developing new strategies for dealing with stress will help you stay clean and free.

A Suggestion

Look at the four causes of stress listed above. When you were smoking, did you use cigarettes to deal with such situations? Now that you are no longer smoking, how are you dealing with them? Identify a specific example of each type of situation from your own life and describe in your journal how you are dealing with it—without cigarettes.

Remember the Advantages of Quitting Smoking

Most people who have quit smoking made several serious attempts before they succeeded. With each attempt, they come a little closer to their goal. Unfortunately, many smokers give up hope of ever being successful and return to smoking. Sometimes they give up because they don't think the advantages of quitting will make up for the discomfort they have to go through. They may not realize that their bodies can repair much of the damage caused by smoking—even by *years* of smoking. After recovering smokers stay clean and free for a few years, the advantages of quitting become clear, and they look back on quitting smoking as one of the most important things they ever did.

A Step in the Right Direction

Has it been hard for you to keep the advantages of quitting in mind? Have you thought about giving up? The years you spent smoking cannot be reclaimed, but you *can* give yourself a healthier future. Over the next few years, your body will repair much of the damage done by tobacco. On the average, quitting smoking will add between five and fifteen years to your life. What do you plan to do with the years you will gain by quitting smoking now?

A Suggestion

Make a list in your journal of the goals you have for the additional years of life recovery will give you.

Recognizing Feelings

From the time they were teenagers, many smokers relied on cigarettes to deal with feelings, and they are poorly prepared to deal with these feelings without cigarettes. When they quit smoking years later, they become overwhelmed with unfamiliar feelings—they may not even be able to name them. They want to quit smoking and hope never to start again, but they fall victim to feelings they cannot comprehend and they relapse.

A Step in the Right Direction

Addictions are never "cured." Every recovering smoker (including you) is at risk for relapse; those who work on improving the quality of their recovery lower their risk of relapse. Understanding how you used cigarettes to help you cope with life will improve the quality of your recovery, because it will help you predict when you are most likely to want a cigarette. Now that you have put some distance between you and your last cigarette, it will be easier for you to identify the feelings that you avoided with the help of a cigarette.

A Suggestion

In your journal, list the feelings that you used smoking to help you deal with: anger, resentment, disappointment, loneliness, embarrassment, confusion, fear, hopelessness, insecurity, inadequacy, boredom, frustration, anxiety, disgust, helplessness, depression, grief, shame, guilt.

Three Strategies for Success

Addiction treatment professionals recommend three specific strategies for their clients: accept the reality of their addiction, eliminate the reminders about chemical use from their lives, and welcome support from others. When alcoholics do these things, their chances of staying sober improve. When cocaine addicts do these things, their chances of staying clean improve. And when recovering smokers do these things, their chances of staying clean and free improve. However, many recovering smokers still imagine that one day they will be able to smoke again *but not get hooked;* they have not completely accepted the reality of their dependence. Some recovering smokers fail to eliminate some obvious relapse triggers: they don't object when people smoke around them, they allow smoking in their homes, and they still keep cigarettes and ashtrays around. And some recovering smokers even hesitate to share their story with other recovering smokers and decline support from others.

A Step in the Right Direction

Have you used the three recovery strategies listed above?

A Suggestion

In your journal, make some notes about how completely you have accepted your nicotine and tobacco dependence, how many associations with smoking you have eliminated, and how actively you have sought support from others and given support to others.

The Hierarchy of Human Needs

Abraham Maslow described what people need to feel whole and complete as "the hierarchy of human needs." The hierarchy follows:

- The most basic needs are *physiological* (needed by our bodies to function), such as food, warmth, and oxygen.
- Once physiological needs are met, we pay attention to our needs for *safety and security.*
- The next level of needs includes *feeling loved* and *belonging to a group.*
- The next most important need is for *self-esteem,* to feel good about ourselves.
- The highest level of needs is *self-actualization,* or becoming all that we can be.

A Step in the Right Direction

How will your recovery meet your human needs?

A Suggestion

Make some notes in your journal about your own needs. How does quitting smoking meet your physiological needs (the needs of your body)? How will quitting help you feel safe and secure? In which ways will it help you feel loved and accepted by others? How will it improve your self-esteem? Finally, how will living your life clean and free help you reach your goals in life, to become the person you want to be?

Share Your Success

Smokers sometimes quit smoking secretly. They don't expect to succeed, so they protect themselves from embarrassment by not telling anyone that they are trying to quit. Smokers who do this usually fail because they are not making a 100 percent effort to quit, and they are not using every available source of support. Success in recovery depends on using every tool and taking advantage of every opportunity. Partial efforts are usually unsuccessful—and being secretive about quitting is an example of a partial effort.

A Step in the Right Direction

Are you proud of your decision to quit smoking? Are you confident you will succeed? Have you purposely not told someone that you are quitting smoking because you would be embarrassed to admit failure to him or her? This is a good time to look at your motivation and willingness to succeed.

A Suggestion

Plan to use every available resource to improve your chances of success. Whom have you avoided talking to about your recovery plans? Why? Are you willing to do whatever it takes to stay clean and free—including telling that person about your recovery program?

Don't Try to Do It Alone

Quitting smoking is hard. Very few smokers can just toss away their cigarettes and quit. Most smokers need to work on it every day, and if they become lazy or complacent, they start smoking again. Quitting smoking is especially hard for people who try to do it all alone. Even people who normally don't like to ask for help discover that accepting help from others in their recovery program is a good idea.

A Step in the Right Direction

Have you asked others to help you in your recovery? Have you hesitated to ask for help? You will be amazed at how willing other people are to support you. Some of these people are recovering smokers themselves, and helping you will help them. One day you may provide the crucial support that another recovering smoker needs to stay clean and free; today, others can provide this support for you. Whom can you accept support from today?

A Suggestion

You can always find—and give—support at a Nicotine Anonymous meeting. For the location of a meeting near you, call the national office of Nicotine Anonymous in San Francisco, at (415) 750-0328. There are no dues or fees at these meetings, no membership lists, and no requirements for membership except one: a desire to stay clean and free from dependence on nicotine and tobacco.

Easy for You to Say

Many people have been able to quit easily and without any special help. "Sure, I quit smoking," they say. "No big deal. One day, I tossed away my cigarettes and I've never smoked since." Many of these people quit smoking ten or twenty years ago, when the evidence of the dangers of smoking first became well known. Some of them were not addicted at all—they just liked to smoke occasionally, just as many people drink a beer occasionally. The majority of smokers today, however, are highly dependent on nicotine and tobacco, and they cannot quit so easily. When they try to quit smoking by throwing away their cigarettes, they soon go out and buy more. Highly dependent smokers must participate in a program of recovery if they intend to stay clean and free.

A Step in the Right Direction

Do you know someone who quit smoking easily or without any help? How do you feel about that person today? Are your feelings about how that person quit smoking influencing your opinion of him or her as a person? If so, your addiction is still controlling you.

A Suggestion

In your journal, describe how nicotine and tobacco dependence has controlled your thoughts and feelings. Does it make you angry? Does it make you resentful? How can you understand your thoughts and feelings better?

When Do You Still Want a Cigarette?

Certain times of the day seem to lend themselves to smoking. Smokers look forward to these times; recovering smokers must be aware that each one is a threat to their recovery. Some of these times include the following: the first thing in the morning, after breakfast, while traveling to work, after lunch, after meetings, at coffee breaks, leaving work, after dinner, after having sex, and the last thing at night.

A Step in the Right Direction

What times of the day were special times for you and your cigarettes? Even though you have not smoked in some time, you may still be tempted to smoke at specific times. Have you noticed when your desire to smoke increases? You cannot change the clock or the calendar, but you can change how you react to situations. The first step in doing so is to become aware of your own relapse triggers.

A Suggestion

In your journal, list the times you once enjoyed smoking. At the end of each day during the next week, rate your desire to smoke in these situations on a scale of one to ten (ten is the strongest; one is the weakest). Soon, you will be able to anticipate how much your desire to smoke will increase in certain situations, and you will be better prepared to deal with your relapse triggers.

Offering Support to Others

Relapses are common in all addictions, including nicotine and tobacco dependence. When recovering smokers relapse, they often reject help from others; this rejection is usually based in shame. After telling people that they had quit smoking, they are often too embarrassed to admit they relapsed. They may become secretive about their smoking, which adds to their feelings of shame—and they keep on smoking.

A Step in the Right Direction

Do you know one or more recovering smokers who have relapsed? Did they appear ashamed or embarrassed? Did they reject help, even when it was offered with genuine concern? They may have been so ashamed of their relapse that they were unwilling to accept help, and they may continue to use cigarettes to deal with their feelings. What could you do to help?

A Suggestion

If relapsed smokers are open to hearing it, share your experience. Remind them that while relapses are common, they do not mean failure; if they can be open and honest about what happened and why it happened, they can get clean and free again. Taking action right away, however, is essential; the longer they continue to smoke, the more difficult it will be for them to quit. If it were you who had relapsed, what offers of help would you be willing to accept?

Guilt, Habit, and Denial

Recovering smokers are often tempted to smoke when a smoker offers them a cigarette. Smokers may make these offers out of guilt, habit, or denial:

- *Guilt.* Most smokers want to quit, and say so, but they don't take the necessary action. Since they know they should quit, they feel guilty about their smoking, and knowing people who *have* quit makes them feel even more guilty.
- *Habit.* Offering a cigarette to a fellow smoker has become an expression of comradeship. Smokers may offer a newly recovering smoker a cigarette out of habit, having done it many times before.
- *Denial.* Many smokers so desperately want to believe that smoking is not addicting that they refuse to accept the truth that recovering smokers cannot smoke again.

A Step in the Right Direction

At some time in the future, a smoker may attempt to sabotage your recovery by offering you a cigarette, saying, "You can probably just have *one*." How will you respond?

A Suggestion

Consider saying "I used to think I could smoke just one, but I've learned that even taking one puff would send me back to smoking, and I prefer to stay clean and free." What other good responses have you thought of?

Time for a Motivation Check

Quitting smoking requires more effort than most people are willing to make. In most surveys, 85 to 90 percent of smokers say they would like to quit, but only 7 percent of smokers actually quit each year, and most of them relapse before the year is up. One of the reasons for this low rate of success is that most people are only willing to make a limited effort, and for a limited time. They start off with enthusiasm and optimism, but when problems arise—mood swings, anxiety, and the constant reminders about smoking—they lose their determination.

A Step in the Right Direction

The Big Book of Alcoholics Anonymous reminds alcoholics who are struggling to stay sober that "half measures availed us nothing," meaning that success requires a full effort, not a partial one. Are you doing everything you possibly can to stay clean and free?

A Suggestion

Give yourself a "motivation check."

- Have you skipped any pages in this book?
- Have you answered every question?
- Have you written your thoughts and feelings in your journal as recommended?
- Have you been satisfied with "half measures" in your recovery program?

What Happened to Humphrey Bogart?

Humphrey Bogart was a great actor who has left us many wonderful films. Watch one; nearly every scene shows Bogie with a cigarette, a pipe, or a cigar. In his films, he uses tobacco to help him play a role. When he smokes one way, he's tough; when he smokes a different way, he's dashing; when he smokes another way, he's strictly business. Tobacco was as much his costar as Lauren Bacall. Bogie continued to make successful films until he died in 1955 at the age of fifty-seven of lung cancer.

A Step in the Right Direction

How did tobacco help you act a role when you were smoking?

- Were you tough, strong, and independent with a cigarette?
- Were you suave or seductive with a cigarette?
- Were you intense or ruthless with a cigarette?
- Were you playful or fun loving with a cigarette?

Did you ever use cigarettes to pretend to be someone you are not? If so, did you expect that a four-inch piece of compost could change your personality?

A Suggestion

Make some notes in your journal about the roles you played with a cigarette. Now that you no longer smoke, you can be the person you really are, all the time. So, who are you?

Thoughts of Smoking Eventually Diminish

Most smokers smoke all day, every day. When given the opportunity, they usually smoke a cigarette about once an hour—or as often as once every twenty minutes. No other drug addicts use chemicals so frequently: alcoholics go several hours or longer without drinking; heroin addicts usually use their drug only two to four times a day; cocaine addicts often go a week or more without using cocaine. By this measure, nicotine is more addicting than alcohol, heroin, or cocaine.

A Step in the Right Direction

When you first started smoking, you only smoked occasionally. When did you start smoking every day? Do you still think about smoking every day? After a while, thoughts of smoking will return less frequently, and soon you will no longer struggle with not smoking on a daily basis. This will make your life more comfortable, but it may lull you into thinking that you are no longer at risk of relapse. Because dependence on nicotine and tobacco is an addiction (and in some ways a more intense addiction than any other), relapse is always a possibility.

A Suggestion

Keep track of how often you think about smoking and the strategies you use to avoid a relapse. You once smoked every day; are you willing to do something for your recovery every day?

Replace Resentments with Gratitude

Research shows that the intensity of nicotine and tobacco dependence varies quite a bit between individual smokers. A few have only minimal nicotine withdrawal symptoms and can quit without help, or with just advice and information. Most, however, cannot quit so easily; they have significant withdrawal symptoms and are at high risk of relapse for many months. Many such recovering smokers express anger at tobacco, at the tobacco companies, and at themselves. And they feel resentful because quitting was so difficult for them.

A Step in the Right Direction

Do you know people who just tossed away their cigarettes and never smoked again? If you could have quit that way, you would have done so long ago. The fact is your dependence on nicotine and tobacco is far too intense for a quick solution. Do you resent people who quit more easily than you? If so, cigarettes are still controlling some of your feelings.

A Suggestion

Release your resentment and focus on being grateful for the progress you have made. Writing a "Good-bye" letter to tobacco can help you replace resentment with gratitude. If you have already written one, pull it out, read it over, and add things that you have learned over the last month. If you have not written one, start today. Start with "Good-bye Tobacco," and tell tobacco why you have left it behind.

Getting Bad News

One of the most dangerous relapse triggers for most recovering smokers is receiving bad news that causes extreme stress. Examples include the following:

- Being in a car crash
- Having a loved one die
- Ending a relationship
- Doing poorly on an examination
- Being audited by the IRS

A Step in the Right Direction

What is the worst news you have gotten since you quit smoking? How did you handle it? What if the news had been even worse than it was? You will get bad news some day, and you may have an urge to smoke—but returning to smoking will only make a bad situation worse. What can you do to handle extreme stress without returning to smoking?

A Suggestion

Always carry your *Keep Quit* chip with you. It symbolizes the hard work you have done in recovery. When you get bad news or are stressed in other ways, hold on to your chip and remember what it stands for. In moments of stress, your chip will remind you to *stay focused* in order to stay *clean and free*.

Drug-Seeking Behavior

One aspect of dependence on any addicting drug is *drug-seeking behavior*—the pattern in which dependent persons obtain and use the drug that they are addicted to. The *Journal of the American Medical Association* recently reported the case of a thirty-six-year-old man, a smoker, who was admitted to a hospital for a gallbladder operation. After the operation, he required oxygen provided by a nasal tube. He wanted to smoke, but his doctor refused to let him because of the oxygen. This man wouldn't take no for an answer, and he snuck a cigarette anyway—with the oxygen running. While he was smoking, his hospital bed caught fire, burning his hand and face, and nearly killing him. Even this experience was not enough to convince him to quit smoking; after he left the hospital, he started smoking again.

A Step in the Right Direction

If you were a friend of this man, what would you tell him about his smoking? What event from your own life would you share with him—some event that demonstrates that you, too, were uncontrollably addicted to nicotine and tobacco?

A Suggestion

Write a brief description in your journal of the personal event in your smoking career that best demonstrates the control that nicotine and tobacco had over you. How does it feel to be released from that control?

Rate Yourself

Addictions (including nicotine and tobacco dependence) and diabetes are similar in many ways: they may be inherited, they are influenced by behavior, they become more of a problem as the individual gets older, and even if the individual's tests are normal at one point (a normal blood sugar or negative drug screen), the disease has not been cured—it is just in remission. If diabetics stop following their diets, their illness takes control again; if recovering people stop working on recovery, their illness takes control again, and they relapse. Preventing relapse must be the primary goal of every person in recovery, regardless of which drug they used—alcohol, cocaine, heroin, or nicotine.

A Step in the Right Direction

Relapses begin when it becomes *possible* to use again, which might be a day or a week before the recovering smoker actually takes that first puff; it could be even longer. Were you in a situation today where it was *possible* for you to smoke again?

A Suggestion

Evaluate your risk of relapse carefully. Here is one way: Every hour during the day, rate yourself on a scale of one to ten, as being closer or further away from a relapse (with ten meaning *ready to relapse*). When your score changes, stop and figure out what made it change. Use your journal to record what you learn about preventing a relapse.

All Your Friends Are Doing It

One of the most common reasons smokers give for deciding to quit smoking is that most of their friends have quit. This reason is *serious* enough for them to quit, but it may not be *personal* enough for them to recover.

A Step in the Right Direction

In order to recover—not just quit smoking—you must make your reasons more personal.

A Suggestion

Respond to the following questions in your journal.

- Did you get your first few cigarettes from friends?
- Do you miss the days when you and your friends smoked together?
- Did you feel isolated from your nonsmoking friends when you were smoking?
- How did you feel when some of your friends who were smokers quit and you didn't?
- Now that you have quit smoking, are your new friends smokers or nonsmokers? If you were still smoking, would they probably be smokers or nonsmokers?
- How will having nonsmoking friends help you stay clean and free?
- How have your opinions about smokers changed since you quit smoking?

Identify the Value of Recovery

When recovering alcoholics, cocaine addicts, and heroin addicts relapse, they endanger their lives, their jobs, and their families. Before long, their world collapses around them. If they do not quit again soon, they are likely to end up in the hospital, in a mental institution, in a prison, or dead. When recovering smokers relapse, however, they rarely experience immediate consequences. They don't lose their jobs; their families don't desert them; they don't get sick; they don't become psychotic; and they don't break any laws. Recovering smokers often fail to devote time and effort to staying clean and free because they do not fear the consequences of a relapse.

A Step in the Right Direction

Have you thought about the consequences of relapsing to smoking? Were you able to rationalize them away, so they didn't sound very serious? Most of the immediate consequences of relapsing to smoking are minor and most of the major ones are far off in the future.

A Suggestion

Identify some significant personal consequences of relapse that you would face right away. For instance, how would you feel about yourself if you relapsed? What kind of a role model would you be for others? On the other hand, how will you feel about yourself when you are clean and free for a year?

Expectations in Recovery

When people make a major change in their lives (like quitting smoking), they expect things to improve. After all, why go through the difficulty of changing if nothing is going to get better? However, the world takes little note of the changes one person makes, and many recovering smokers have inappropriate expectations of how the future will be.

A Step in the Right Direction

Were you expecting a lot of good things to result from your quitting smoking? Were you disappointed when you realized that some of the changes you hoped for were not going to happen? When you were still smoking, you could share your sorrows with a cigarette, but now that you have quit smoking, what will you do? Have you thought about smoking again?

A Suggestion

On your next really bad day, open your journal and turn to a fresh page. Start with a sentence that summarizes your day, such as "Today was a bad day because I was blamed for something that wasn't my fault." If you felt like smoking, start your next sentence with "I wanted a cigarette because. . . ." Would smoking have helped solve the problem? Would smoking have made your day better? No matter how bad your day was, smoking again would only have made it worse. Describe your feelings, and finish with this sentence: "If I started smoking again over this problem. . . ."

Smoking Causes Cancer

According to the surgeon general, smoking leads to the deaths of over 400,000 Americans every year, most of whom die from cancer. There are over 4,000 chemicals in cigarette smoke; many of these chemicals are known to cause cancer, including nitrosamines, pyrethrins, benzene, radon, and cadmium. Most people know that smoking causes lung cancer, but many are unaware that it also increases the risk of getting cancer of the cervix, breast, pancreas, bladder, stomach, colon, mouth, and tongue. Cancers begin painlessly, with the mutation of a single cell. The cancer grows slowly until it reaches a certain size, and then it spreads to other parts of the body. Of the known causes of cancer, smoking is the most important one that people can do something about. Quitting smoking greatly reduces a person's risk of getting cancer.

A Step in the Right Direction

Have you been concerned that you might get cancer because of your smoking? Have you known someone who did? Here's the good news: now that you are not smoking, your risk of getting cancer will gradually decrease, and in a few years it will reach the level of people who have never smoked.

A Suggestion

Take a good look at your overall health. Now that you are not smoking, what other changes are you considering to improve your health?

Relapse Triggers Are Everywhere

Smokers build up many associations between things they see and smoking. Some examples include

- Seeing someone smoking
- Seeing a pack of cigarettes on a table
- Passing a display of tobacco products in a store
- Seeing "No Smoking" signs
- Seeing cigarette smoke—or any smoke, for that matter

A Step in the Right Direction

Visual cues about smoking can be powerful triggers for you, even if you have been clean and free for months. Finding a pack of cigarettes in a drawer or in the pocket of a seldom-worn coat can make you want to smoke one. Have you seen something lately that reminded you of smoking? Have you seen a favorite ashtray, lighter, or cigarette case? What will you do when you see something that makes you want to smoke?

A Suggestion
(though not an easy one)

Whenever you find something that reminds you of smoking, throw it away immediately—regardless of its value. If it could trigger a relapse, how much is it really worth?

Other People's Smoking

Many smokers automatically reach for a cigarette when they see someone else light up. There is something about seeing someone else smoke that triggers the desire for a cigarette. For some people, this remains a relapse trigger for years after they quit smoking. Even though they no longer smoke and don't want to smoke, seeing someone else smoking automatically causes them to touch their pocket or reach for their handbag as if they were reaching for their cigarettes.

A Step in the Right Direction

When you were still smoking, did you reach for your cigarettes when you saw someone else smoking? If so, you may be in danger of automatically saying "Hey, let me have one of those" whenever you see someone else smoking. What can you do to eliminate this threat to your recovery?

A Suggestion

In your journal, make a list of your visual cues to smoking, such as seeing someone with a pack of cigarettes, seeing someone light up, or seeing someone smoking. Look for these situations during the day. At the end of the day, rate how much pressure to smoke you felt in each situation. When you make this feeling conscious instead of automatic, you will begin to eliminate this relapse trigger from your life.

Share Your Understanding of Recovery

Relapses are common in all addictions, including nicotine and tobacco dependence. In order to avoid a relapse, recovering smokers often must do things they never thought they could. Reaching out to people they do not know well is an example. When recovering smokers help other people quit smoking, they all benefit; by sharing their knowledge of recovery, they help themselves as well as others. However, many recovering smokers are reluctant to reach out to others because they don't want to seem intrusive or to embarrass anyone.

A Step in the Right Direction

Did someone's advice, support, or encouragement help you make the decision to quit smoking? Did someone help you through some of the rough spots in the first few weeks after you quit?

A Suggestion

Identify several times in the first few months of your recovery when a guiding hand could have been helpful to you. What questions did you have that you hesitated to ask? Now that you have been clean and free for several months, you know many of the answers. Your experience could make the difference between success and relapse for another person. Have you lent a hand to someone who is trying to quit smoking? Do you know someone who could use your support?

Your Body Has Already Started to Heal

After people quit smoking, their bodies begin to heal. Here are some health improvements recovering smokers experience:

- Bronchitis (infection in the breathing passages leading to the lungs) improves within a week as the lungs clear out the infected mucus.
- The risk of developing lung cancer begins to decline within two years and continues to decline for about ten years.
- The risk of having a stroke begins to decline after five years.
- The risk of having a heart attack starts to decline as soon as the smoker quits, and within three years, the recovering smoker has the same risk of having a heart attack as people of the same age who never smoked.

A Step in the Right Direction

Which smoking-related diseases were you afraid you might get?

A Suggestion

Each day this week, choose one part of your body that smoking can damage (lungs, sinuses, throat, heart, brain, stomach, skin). Focus on that part of your body and see if you can tell how it feels. You are already healthier than you were when you were smoking; can you feel the difference? In your journal, describe in words or draw a picture to show how your body is healing.

Unreasonable Expectations

George Bernard Shaw once wrote, "The reasonable man adapts himself to the world; the unreasonable one persists in trying to adapt the world to himself. Therefore, all progress depends on the unreasonable man."

A Step in the Right Direction

Was it unreasonable for your family and friends to expect you to quit smoking? Is it unreasonable to expect that you will remain smokefree for the rest of your life? Is it unreasonable to expect other smokers to quit smoking too? An *unreasonable* expectation is one that ordinary, average people have no hope of meeting. George Bernard Shaw says that the hope of the world rests on people who go beyond reasonable expectations, who focus their determination on meeting difficult challenges.

A Suggestion

Decide today if you will be satisfied with being ordinary or if you intend to achieve worthwhile goals in your life. Answer these questions in your journal:

- Are you willing to do whatever it takes to stay clean and free?
- Are you willing to stand up for your right to breathe clean, smokefree air?
- Are you willing to insist that the tobacco companies stop promoting their products to children?

How Addicting Is Nicotine?

Dr. Jack Henningfield and Dr. Neal Benowitz, two of the most prominent researchers on addictions in the United States, recently compared nicotine with heroin, cocaine, alcohol, caffeine, and marijuana in terms of the strength of the dependency the chemical causes and the severity of withdrawal. By *dependence,* they meant the ability of the drug to control the user's thoughts, feelings, and behavior, and the difficulty users have in quitting. Both scientists rated nicotine dependence as more intense than dependence on any of the other five drugs. By *withdrawal,* they meant the severity of the symptoms that occur when an addicted user stops using the chemical. Both scientists rated alcohol withdrawal as the most severe; they rated nicotine withdrawal as about the same as cocaine withdrawal.

A Step in the Right Direction

You probably didn't need two scientists to tell you that quitting smoking was difficult. But did you realize that experts in the field rate nicotine dependence as more intense than heroin, cocaine, or alcohol dependence? Did you realize that they consider nicotine withdrawal to be just as severe as cocaine withdrawal?

A Suggestion

Write down some examples of how your nicotine and tobacco dependence controlled your thoughts, feelings, and behavior.

You Are Known by the Company You Keep

In 1950, gender was the main factor separating smokers from nonsmokers: men smoked, women didn't. Today, so many men have quit smoking and so many young women are starting to smoke that the sexes have similar smoking rates—27 percent for men and 23 percent for women. Education has become the most important factor separating smokers from nonsmokers: 38 percent of high school dropouts smoke, but only 15 percent of college graduates smoke. Among teenagers, twice as many high school dropouts smoke as do teenagers who stay in school. In 1950, nearly half of all physicians smoked cigarettes; today only 3 percent of physicians smoke.

A Step in the Right Direction

When you were a smoker, nonsmokers considered you an uneducated person, whether you were or not. Now that you are no longer smoking, many people will consider you to be a more intelligent person.

A Suggestion

Make some notes in your journal about how your attitude toward smokers has changed since you quit smoking. How has your attitude about yourself changed now that you are clean and free?

Cigarettes Help Smokers Socialize

Cigarettes provide smokers with an opportunity to socialize. Years ago, the men would sit around smoking pipes or cigars and exclude the women. Public buildings and larger homes had "smoking rooms" that only men were allowed to use. In 1968, only 8 percent of women smoked; in that year, the Philip Morris Company started advertising Virginia Slims by showing "liberated women" smoking and the motto "You've come a long way, baby." By 1974, 14 percent of women smoked, while the number of male smokers was decreasing. Today, almost as many women smoke as do men, and men and women routinely smoke while socializing together. Smokers gather together in little groups outside nonsmoking buildings to smoke like campers clustered around a campfire, with its fire and smoke, and its security and feeling of belonging. When smokers quit, they not only give up smoking but also some of their security and some of their friends.

A Step in the Right Direction

Do you miss your smoking friends and the times you smoked together? How do you spend the time you used to spend smoking?

A Suggestion

Describe for your journal how you used cigarettes to help you socialize. Now that you no longer smoke, whom do you socialize with? How has quitting affected your other relationships?

Reward Yourself for Staying Clean and Free

Smokers often treat their cigarettes as rewards for completing a project, closing a sale, surviving a crisis, or just making it through another day. All day, they look forward to settling back with a cigarette. They think about the smell and the texture and the taste of a cigarette; they anticipate how they will feel as the smoke fills their lungs and the nicotine enters their brains. When the reward finally comes, it is just as satisfying as they hoped it would be. The tobacco comforts them, the smoke soothes them, and the nicotine stimulates them. What a splendid reward! After they quit smoking, recovering smokers no longer have cigarettes to reward themselves with, to relax with, or to look forward to. They must find other rewards in order to stay clean and free.

A Step in the Right Direction

When you were still smoking, did you reward yourself with cigarettes? Were your successes sweeter because you celebrated them with a cigarette? How can you reward yourself in other ways?

A Suggestion

Regardless of what else you have done, your greatest success this week has been *not smoking*. You deserve a reward for this success. Take half the money you would have spent on cigarettes this week and spend it on a treat for yourself. What would you like to do with the other half?

The Process of Recovery

Smokers spend years addicted to nicotine and tobacco, and then spend years getting ready to quit. After they quit, they go through several distinct phases in their first year of recovery:

- They spend the first few weeks focused on *just not smoking.*
- After they become a little more comfortable with being a nonsmoker, they begin to think about living a smokefree life.
- When they begin to feel secure in their recovery, they begin to think about what they can do to help other people quit smoking.
- Eventually, they want to reach out and help prevent young people from starting to smoke in the first place.

A Step in the Right Direction

Where are you today in this process?

A Suggestion

Work on your own addiction first. If you are still struggling to stay clean and free, it's too early to be reaching out to others in a big way. But when you are ready, see if there is a smokefree coalition in your area, or a branch of the American Cancer Society or the American Lung Association. Call them and let them know that you have successfully quit smoking and that you are ready to help others do the same. You will help yourself by helping others.

Three Approaches to Recovery

Psychologists have been developing smoking cessation methods for at least thirty years; most of their methods rely on *cognitive and behavioral* strategies (cutting down gradually, substituting alternative behaviors, identifying relapse triggers, and switching brands). Medical doctors have been working on smoking cessation methods for only about fifteen years; most of their methods rely on *medication* (nicotine gum, nicotine patch, clonidine, and antidepressants). Only in the last five to ten years have addiction treatment professionals begun to work on nicotine dependence; they focus on helping smokers *understand the nature of nicotine and tobacco dependence.*

A Step in the Right Direction

This book incorporates elements of all three approaches to recovery from nicotine and tobacco dependence. Have you benefited from the *cognitive and behavioral strategies?* Did you use *medication* to help you through nicotine withdrawal? Has this book helped you *understand your dependence* better?

A Suggestion

Design the ideal recovery program for you, incorporating elements of all three approaches. Which activities would you include? What emphasis would you place on each one? How would you vary the emphasis over the first year of recovery?

Making Decisions

Relapses are common in all addictions, including nicotine and tobacco dependence. When recovering smokers relapse, they often smoke for a long time, undecided about trying to quit again. Their friends and family know they are smoking and can see no evidence that they are trying to quit. But within these relapsed smokers, a struggle rages between the part of them that wants to quit again and the part that is afraid to make another effort. They may not show it, but they are worried, tense, and ashamed. Unfortunately, they quickly discover that smoking helps them cope with these turbulent emotions, and they can become even more dependent on their cigarettes.

A Step in the Right Direction

Do you understand the feelings that relapsed smokers have? What could you do to encourage a relapsed smoker to decide to quit again?

A Suggestion

Share your personal story with a relapsed smoker, emphasizing why you decided to quit smoking. Describe how you dealt with the struggle between the part of you that wanted to quit and the part of you that was afraid to try. Now that you have been clean and free for some time, do you still question whether or not you made the right decision?

Reduce Your Urge to Smoke Again

Some smokers quit and never even consider smoking again, but most continue to think (and dream) about smoking. These notions are no more than passing thoughts for most recovering smokers, but others cannot stop thinking about smoking. Even ten or twenty years after their last cigarette, many recovering smokers still think about smoking every day. They still turn their head when they smell someone smoking and they still long for a cigarette. Even though they don't act on these thoughts, they are still being controlled by cigarettes.

A Step in the Right Direction

Have you thought about smoking today? It is normal to still be thinking about smoking on a regular basis during the first year after quitting. Did you wonder what a cigarette would taste like today? Did you seriously consider smoking again today? If you did, you must take action to prevent a relapse, or your longing for a cigarette may grow to an irresistible craving that will overwhelm you.

A Suggestion

Defeat your urge to smoke again before it grows any stronger. When you next enter a situation in which you think you might want to smoke, tell someone there that, yes, you *do* want to smoke, but that you have decided not to. In this way, you will reduce your risk of relapse and make the situation safer.

Cigarette Smoking in the Movies

In the first half of the twentieth century, cigarette smoking was considered sophisticated for men and a bit daring for women. This is evident in the movies of the era. Humphrey Bogart smoked a cigarette or a cigar or a pipe in every one of his movies; in *To Have and Have Not* (1944), he showed how suave he was by lighting Lauren Bacall's cigarette for her. Paul Henreid did even better in *Now, Voyager* (1942), when he lit a cigarette for himself and one for Bette Davis at the same time. Bogart and Henreid helped create an image of smoking as a manly thing to do; Bacall and Davis helped create an image of smoking as something that bold, fearless women did. (A few years after making these pictures, both Humphrey Bogart and Paul Henreid died of cancer.)

A Step in the Right Direction

What do you think of when you see movie stars or other famous people smoking? Did seeing a celebrity smoke influence you to start smoking? Research shows that children think positively about smoking when they see their role models smoking. Did you influence a young person to start smoking? What can you do to be a different kind of role model now?

A Suggestion

Volunteer to speak about the dangers of smoking at a school or for a church group. Use your experience to help others.

Passive Smoke Is Dangerous

Smokers affect the health of those around them as well as their own health. Nonsmokers (both adults and children) absorb nicotine, carbon particles, carcinogens, and other toxic chemicals when they breathe smoke-filled air. The 1991 surgeon general's report states that children of smokers have twice as many respiratory illnesses each year as the children of nonsmokers. Passive smoke kills 53,000 adults in the U.S. each year; 3,000 of these deaths are due to lung cancer and most of the rest are due to heart disease. Pregnant women who smoke pass toxic chemicals to their unborn children. Even nonsmoking pregnant women exposed to passive smoke absorb enough toxic chemicals to affect the health of their babies.

A Step in the Right Direction

Have you become more aware of passive smoke since you quit smoking? Most recovering smokers become very sensitive to it; some find the smell disgusting and some find it attractive. How have you dealt with passive smoke since you quit smoking?

A Suggestion

Start calling it "smoke pollution" instead of passive smoke, and use the term "involuntary smoking" to describe what you have to do when someone is smoking near you. How do you feel about smokers polluting the air you breathe? How do you feel about the smoke pollution you were responsible for in the past?

Be Prepared to Deal with Emergencies

Some relapses are planned; some are predictable; but many others are the result of impulsiveness. Smokers often relapse without warning in certain situations, such as when they feel stressed or anxious, in an emergency, or after a personal tragedy.

A Step in the Right Direction

Here are some situations where impulse relapses occur.

- You are at a party, having a great time. You have had a drink or two and then the person you are talking to lights a cigarette and extends the pack to you, saying, "Want one?"
- You are preparing for an important family event and are at your wit's end because you can't find something you need. You rummage through your drawers and can't find it—but suddenly you come across an old pack of cigarettes and a lighter that must have been there for months. "Oh, why not," you say. "It'll help me calm down."
- You are in a car crash. Everyone gets out of the damaged cars and someone lights a cigarette. Before you even think about it, you say, "Here—give me one of those."

A Suggestion

Imagine a similar situation that could happen to you and describe it in your journal.

Taking Responsibility

Some recovering smokers who relapse use the word "slip" to imply that their relapse was someone else's fault, that they fell victim to pressure or to someone else's encouragement to smoke. They don't want to take responsibility for their behavior. Recovery from any addiction requires that individuals take responsibility for their lives and their actions.

A Step in the Right Direction

Have you ever blamed someone else for "making" you smoke? Did you ever quit smoking, and then relapse under stress and say, "I didn't have any other choice"? If so, you did not accept responsibility for your actions. Is it possible that you set yourself up for a relapse? Recovery from dependence on nicotine and tobacco demands an honest self-evaluation of the times you intended to quit smoking, but failed. "Slip" could stand for "Something Lousy I Planned." Many recovering smokers unintentionally put themselves in situations where their relapse risk is high—and then wonder why they relapsed. Has this happened to you in the past?

A Suggestion

Ask other recovering smokers if they see you setting yourself up for a relapse. If they say yes, accept the responsibility for changing your behavior. Are you doing everything you need to do, every day, to stay clean and free?

Dealing with Anxiety

Anxiety is a part of everyday life; no one can escape it. Research shows that smokers, as a group, are no more anxious than nonsmokers but that smokers use cigarettes to deal with anxiety (while nonsmokers develop other ways of dealing with it). After quitting, smokers have to learn new ways of dealing with anxiety or they will return to smoking when they feel anxious.

A Step in the Right Direction

Are you frequently anxious and tense? Are you more anxious and tense than you were when you were smoking? Have there been times when you felt you just couldn't take it anymore and you'd either explode or go crazy if you didn't smoke? These are common feelings recovering smokers have just before they break down and smoke. What other options do you have?

A Suggestion

Some people put off dealing with problems and anxieties, hoping they will go away. They usually don't go away, but just keep getting worse. If you wait too long, the anxiety may become overwhelming or it may be too late to do anything about it. Instead of waiting and hoping for the perfect solution, learn to deal with problems as they develop. Is there a situation in your life right now that could get out of hand if you don't deal with it?

Being Considerate

One of the most common reasons smokers give for deciding to quit smoking is to be more considerate of others, particularly those with respiratory problems. This reason is *serious* enough for them to quit, but it may not be *personal* enough for them to recover.

A Step in the Right Direction

In order to recover—not just quit smoking—you must make your reasons more personal.

A Suggestion

Respond to the following questions in your journal.

- Do you have friends or relatives with asthma, bronchitis, emphysema, or respiratory allergies? Has their breathing ever been affected by other people's smoking?
- Have you had respiratory problems yourself? Has your breathing ever been affected by other people's smoking?
- Did your smoking ever cause or worsen someone's asthma, bronchitis, emphysema, pneumonia, respiratory allergies, or lung cancer?
- What do you do now when someone's cigarette smoke bothers you?
- What kind of nonsmoker will you be: aggressive or sympathetic, assertive or timid, open or secretive?

Be One of the Winners

Research shows that 85 percent of smokers say they would like to quit, but only 20 percent plan to quit in the next year. Of those who plan to quit, only one-third actually make a serious attempt to quit smoking in the next year, and most of them start smoking again. Doctors, public health specialists, educators, and psychologists are working on techniques to improve these low success rates. The percentage of smokers who say they plan to quit has increased as a result of public education about the dangers of smoking. Doctors help their patients quit by prescribing the nicotine patch. Psychologists have developed more effective smoking cessation programs and public health specialists have made them more accessible. New relapse-prevention materials (like this program) seek to reduce the high relapse rate among recovering smokers. These efforts have already produced positive results.

A Step in the Right Direction

You are one of a growing number of people who have quit smoking and are taking action to avoid relapse. You probably know of people who quit smoking and later relapsed. You can benefit from their experiences.

A Suggestion

Identify a number of reasons why *other people* have relapsed. What are you doing to eliminate those threats to recovery in your own life?

Guided Imagery Exercise

Use guided imagery to help you relax, focus on recovery, and help your body heal.

A Step in the Right Direction

Guided imagery is a valuable strategy for relaxing your body while focusing the power of your mind. Here is a guided imagery exercise you can use; you will find others as you move through this book.

Plan to do this exercise for about five minutes. Sit in a comfortable chair or lie down, legs and arms uncrossed. Close your eyes, and breathe slowly and deeply. With each deep breath, imagine yourself becoming more and more relaxed. Focus on your breathing. Continue to breathe deeply, allowing all the concerns of the day to leave your mind as the air leaves your lungs. When your body is thoroughly relaxed, turn your attention to your lungs. Search through your lungs, looking in every tiny crevice and corner. Find the cells that have been most damaged by cigarette smoke—these are the ones most likely to turn cancerous. Mark them in some way, and call your body's white blood cells—the tumor fighters—to eradicate these dangerous cells. Continue to breathe deeply and relax. After about five minutes, open your eyes and notice how you feel.

A Suggestion

Use guided imagery every day to help your body and your mind heal.

The Sooner the Better

Relapses are common in all addictions, including nicotine and tobacco dependence. When recovering alcoholics relapse, they often feel that there is no point in making another effort; when recovering smokers relapse, they often feel that way too. These people become overwhelmed with a feeling of helplessness, which completely drains their energy. Recovering smokers who feel helpless have allowed their addiction to take complete control. With each cigarette, they develop more tolerance, a deeper dependence, and more fear about quitting again. The longer they smoke, the harder it becomes to stop. Many relapsed smokers never make another attempt to quit smoking and continue to smoke until they die.

A Step in the Right Direction

Do you know one or more recovering smokers who have relapsed? What can you do to help?

A Suggestion

Encourage them to make another effort to quit *right away.* The longer they smoke, the harder it will be for them to quit again. What words of encouragement might a relapsed smoker who feels helpless accept? If it were you who had relapsed, what kind of support would *you* be willing to accept? In your journal, list some of the words of encouragement you think *you* would like to hear in a similar situation.

Avoid High-Risk Situations

Overconfidence is frequently a problem for recovering smokers. After not smoking for a while, they sometimes forget that nicotine and tobacco dependence is a lifelong illness that is never cured. As urges to smoke become less frequent, some recovering smokers unintentionally place themselves in high-risk situations—or worse, they decide to "test themselves" by going to a place where people are smoking to prove that they can handle the temptation. This has led to the relapse of many recovering smokers.

A Step in the Right Direction

Do you wish you were "cured" of your nicotine and tobacco dependence? Have you wanted to test yourself (to prove how much control you have)? Have you found yourself in other situations where you might have smoked? If so, cigarettes are still controlling your thoughts, feelings, and actions, even though you are no longer smoking. When cigarettes no longer control you, such thoughts will no longer enter your mind.

A Suggestion

You can improve your chances of staying clean and free by writing a "Good-bye" letter to tobacco. If you have already written one, pull it out, read it over, and add things that you have learned in the last month. If you have not written one, start today. Start with "Good-bye Tobacco," and tell tobacco why you have left it behind.

What Did Smoking Do for You?

Smokers often do not realize how much they got out of smoking until they quit. When asked why they smoke, smokers often say, "It relaxes me" or "I just like to smoke." After they quit, they suddenly discover how often they used smoking to help them cope with stress. They also discover that they used cigarettes to help them handle anger, fear, anxiety, frustration, embarrassment, sorrow, boredom, and loneliness—and that dealing with these uncomfortable feelings without a cigarette is surprisingly difficult.

A Step in the Right Direction

Did you use smoking to help you deal with certain feelings? How have you dealt with these feelings since you quit smoking? Did you use smoking to help you cope with stress? How have you handled stress since you quit smoking?

A Suggestion

Make a list in your journal of the feelings and emotions that you once dealt with by smoking. Next to each item on the list, write down one way you have learned to deal with that feeling or emotion without smoking. Then write down several stressful situations that once made you want to smoke; next to each one, write down how you have handled that situation without smoking. Which strategies have worked best for you? You're still clean and free—so you must be doing something right.

Understanding Addiction

Most people do not understand addictive diseases, especially nicotine and tobacco dependence. Recovering smokers do not necessarily understand the nature of nicotine and tobacco dependence any better than a person who never smoked. Smokers often say, "I can't quit," but they *can*. Neversmokers often ask, "Why don't smokers just quit?" because they don't understand how difficult quitting smoking really is. Many former smokers say, "I quit smoking, so I know what works. Here's what *you* have to do . . . ," but they don't realize that strategies that work for one person may not work for another.

A Step in the Right Direction

How would you encourage a demoralized smoker to make another effort to quit? How would you explain to a neversmoker the overwhelming control that cigarettes have over smokers? How would you explain to an aggressive former smoker that all smokers are not alike and that each one needs to direct a personal program of recovery?

A Suggestion

Test out your answers to these three questions by finding a smoker, a neversmoker, or a recovering smoker who has expressed interest in your recovery. Explain to that person how dependence on nicotine and tobacco has affected you.

Relapse Situations

Recovering smokers remain at risk for relapse their entire lives. Nearly nine out of ten recovering smokers relapse in the first year after quitting. Even twenty or more years after quitting, a certain number of recovering smokers return to smoking, usually because of emotional stress or because they associate smoking with the situation they are in.

A Step in the Right Direction

You may be tempted to smoke again during your first year of recovery. Typical relapse situations in the first year after quitting include the following:

- While watching an emotional show on TV
- While watching your team lose an important game
- After breaking up with a boyfriend or girlfriend
- After losing a job
- After being in a car crash
- During a divorce
- After suffering the death or illness of a friend or relative

Which of these situations might put you at risk of relapse?

A Suggestion

Imagine how you would handle each of these situations and write down your ideas in your journal.

Acknowledging the Desire to Smoke Again

Even years after smoking their last cigarette, many recovering smokers report that they frequently think about the pleasures of smoking. Their desire to smoke increases and decreases, depending on the situation, their emotions, and many other factors. When the desire to smoke increases, they are at the greatest risk of relapse; if they are offered a cigarette at that moment, they may be taken by surprise and accept one before they realize it.

A Step in the Right Direction

Since you quit smoking, have you experienced moments when you really wanted a cigarette? What would have happened if someone had offered you a cigarette at that moment? Some people have an uncanny ability to know what you're thinking. They may offer you a cigarette unexpectedly, saying, "I can tell you really want a cigarette, don't you?" (And of course, they're right.) At that moment, you are at risk of thinking, "Oh, well, if it's so obvious to everyone, I might as well go ahead and smoke." Can you imagine being in such a situation? How would you respond?

A Suggestion

Consider acknowledging how you feel by saying, "It's true, I really do want a cigarette" and then state your intentions by saying, "But I've decided that staying clean and free is more important." What other good responses have you thought of?

Stay Focused on Recovery

Seeing a cigarette and seeing cigarette smoke are serious relapse triggers for a recovering smoker, but an even more dangerous trigger is seeing smokers enjoying themselves as they inhale, blow out the smoke, smile, and relax.

A Step in the Right Direction

You may have a tremendous craving to smoke when you see someone smoking. The cigarette, the smoke, and the satisfaction on the face of the smoker can all attract your attention like a magnet and remind you of smoking. At moments like these, you need to focus your attention on *recovery* and you must do it right away. Every second that you spend focusing on smoking draws you closer to a relapse.

A Suggestion

Find something to focus on that reminds you of recovery—the change in your pocket that you used to spend on cigarettes, your clean fingers, your fresh breath, or your clear lungs. If you always carry your *Keep Quit!* chip with you, you will have a reminder of your goal near at hand. Tell yourself over and over: "Stay focused." When you do this, the desire to smoke will fade.

Should You Quit to Please Your Family?

One of the most common reasons smokers give for deciding to quit smoking is because their families want them to quit. This reason is *serious* enough for them to quit, but it may not be *personal* enough for them to recover.

A Step in the Right Direction

In order to recover—not just quit smoking—you must make your reasons more personal.

A Suggestion

Respond to the following questions in your journal.

- Consider each person in your family individually. Which ones have asked you to quit smoking? How did you respond at the time?
- Did the smoke from your cigarettes harm any members of your family?
- Did your smoking ever provoke arguments with your family members?
- Did you ever spend time smoking instead of spending time with your family (such as leaving the family to go outside to smoke)?
- Did you influence any children in your family to start smoking?
- What kind of role model will you be for your family now that you are clean and free?

Think It Through

After they first quit smoking, most recovering smokers think about smoking every day—sometimes dozens of times a day. These thoughts become less intense and less frequent as time passes, but they may last for weeks or even months in some individuals. Some recovering smokers desperately want to stay clean and free, but they get worn down by constantly thinking how nice it would be to smoke. Eventually, many relapse.

A Step in the Right Direction

Have you been thinking about smoking? What can you do to improve your chances of staying clean and free?

A Suggestion

The next time you think about smoking again, thoroughly think through what the consequences would be.

- If you had smoked today, how would your body feel tomorrow morning? How would your head, your mouth, and your tongue feel?
- If you had smoked today, what would you tell the people at work? How would they react?
- If you had smoked today, what would you tell your family members? How would they react?
- If you had smoked today, how would you feel about yourself right now?

Are You Slipping Back into Denial?

Recovering smokers can easily talk themselves into smoking again. They might say to themselves, "One won't hurt" or "I don't feel all that much better since I quit smoking—what's the point?" or "I'll just switch to a low-tar brand." These statements indicate that the recovering smoker is slipping back into denial, an unconscious defense against accepting the truth.

A Step in the Right Direction

Have you caught yourself thinking about smoking again and making excuses that would justify it? Have you heard your "denial voice" talking to you? If you have, it means that your dependence on nicotine and tobacco is trying to take control again—and it will succeed unless you take action to prevent it. What can you do to take back control of your thoughts?

A Suggestion

Put your clean and free voice back in charge. Give yourself one of these messages:

- "I really do miss smoking, but I'm going to stay focused on recovery."
- "One cigarette is too many and a thousand won't be enough."
- "If I smoke today, what will I tell my family tomorrow?"
- "I'm clean and free."

Cigarettes Help Teenagers Deal with Their Feelings

Teenagers are intrigued by smoking. They see adults and other teenagers smoking, and they believe that smoking will make them feel older and more mature. Their first cigarette is usually a gift from a friend; within a year of their first cigarette, most teenagers are smoking daily. This takes practice, because inhaling caustic smoke is not a normal behavior. Soon, however, cigarettes become their constant companions. When they have to deal with rejection, loneliness, embarrassment, and feelings of inadequacy, cigarettes help them feel normal and part of the crowd.

A Step in the Right Direction

When you were a teenager, did you use cigarettes to help you deal with rejection, loneliness, embarrassment, and feelings of inadequacy? When you turned to cigarettes, did they deliver as expected? Cigarettes were once your friends, right there when you needed them. Now that you are no longer smoking, how have you dealt with these situations?

A Suggestion

Identify specific examples of when you relied on cigarettes to deal with rejection, loneliness, embarrassment, and feelings of inadequacy. In your journal, describe how cigarettes helped you. Following each description, make some notes on how you have been coping with these feelings now that you are clean and free.

Identifying Your Self-Defeating Behaviors

Most people do a few things that repeatedly cause them problems; psychologists call these "self-defeating behaviors." While most people have difficulty recognizing their own self-defeating behaviors, it is possible to identify them and change them. But it's not easy.

A Step in the Right Direction

What are some of your self-defeating behaviors?

- Are you the kind of person who takes action quickly (sometimes too quickly), or are you the kind of person who waits until all the information is in (and sometimes waits too long)?
- Are you the kind of person who never asks advice (and is too proud to admit you might be wrong), or are you the kind of person who gets opinions from everyone (and doesn't give yourself credit for having good ideas of your own)?
- Are you the kind of person who tackles problems with confidence (even when you don't really know what you're doing), or are you the kind of person who avoids getting started (even though you know how to do it)?

A Suggestion

Identify a self-defeating behavior that could prevent you from staying clean and free. Who could help you identify self-defeating behaviors that you cannot recognize?

Develop an "Attitude of Gratitude"

Many people take their families, their friends, and even their lives for granted; they don't appreciate what they have until they lose it. Taking recovery for granted can set recovering people up for relapse. Recovering people in Alcoholics Anonymous speak about the importance of developing an "attitude of gratitude," whereby they appreciate their sobriety, the AA program, and the people who support them. This kind of attitude helps them value what they have accomplished and improves their chances of maintaining recovery.

A Step in the Right Direction

Have you taken your recovery from dependence on tobacco and nicotine for granted? After the discomfort of withdrawal has passed, many recovering smokers forget how difficult quitting was. They may minimize the importance of the support they received in quitting. One day, they may no longer see their recovery as important. Have you begun to think this way?

A Suggestion

Work on developing an attitude of gratitude. Are you grateful that you no longer suffer the symptoms of nicotine withdrawal? Are you grateful for the support you have received? Have you gone back to those people who supported you to express your gratitude? Are you grateful for the opportunity to add years to your life and quality to those years? How can you show gratitude that you are clean and free today?

Your Recovery Threatens Someone's Smoking

When one member of a group of smokers quits smoking, he or she usually leaves the group. Recovering smokers rarely feel comfortable in the company of smokers, and even if the other group members remain friendly, their friendship usually dwindles away. The remaining members of the group tend to pull together to protect their smoking. The fact that one of them could quit threatens the others' smoking; it reminds them of their failure to quit and makes them feel guilty.

A Step in the Right Direction

Your recovery from dependence on nicotine and tobacco represents a threat to your friends' smoking. When they see that you are no longer smoking, they have three choices:

- They can quit, too (which is very hard).
- They can pretend you were never really a part of their group (hard, but not impossible).
- They can entice you to start smoking again. (Hard or easy? It depends on you.)

A Suggestion

Consider the friends you once smoked with. How will they deal with the fact that you no longer smoke? How will you deal with no longer being part of their circle?

Make a Break with the Past

Smokers can harm others by their smoking. This harm may be due directly to smoking (such as physical damage done to non-smokers who inhale smoke from the environment), indirectly due to smoking (such as damage to furniture from a burning cigarette), or a result of their dependency (such as smokers who put off taking care of their children until they finish smoking their cigarette). In recovery, recovering smokers can repair much of the damage done to their relationships by making amends to the individuals they harmed. This is very difficult to do and most recovering smokers put it off—sometimes forever. However, experience has shown that making amends is a good way of breaking with the past to create a new future—a clean and free future.

A Step in the Right Direction

Have you thought about the harm you may have caused others by smoking? Are you ready to move to the next level in your recovery?

A Suggestion

In your journal, list all the people you may have harmed by your smoking. Identify how your smoking harmed each person and how it affected your relationship. Think about how you would like to make amends to each person on your list, and make some notes about how you would consider doing this.

Feeling Proud

One of the most common reasons smokers give for deciding to quit smoking is that they want to do something they can be proud of. This reason is *serious* enough for them to quit, but it may not be *personal* enough for them to recover.

A Step in the Right Direction

In order to recover—not just quit smoking—you must make your reasons more personal.

A Suggestion

Respond to the following questions in your journal.

- How did you feel about yourself when you first started smoking? How did becoming a smoker change your image of yourself?
- How did you feel when your friends quit smoking but you didn't?
- Did you ever promise someone that you would quit smoking, while fully intending to continue smoking? If so, how did that make you feel?
- Did your self-confidence improve when you finally put out your last cigarette? Did it improve even more when you were clean and free for thirty days?
- How does your recovery compare with other accomplishments in your life?
- How do you feel about yourself, now that you are clean and free?

Cigarettes Became Your Lover

Smokers develop a special relationship with their cigarettes. After years of being a friend, cigarettes become a smoker's lover. Cigarettes are patient, nurturing, and quiet; they are always available, willing, and consistent—much better than most lovers. In moments of stress, smokers learn that they can turn to a cigarette and never be disappointed. Many smokers become more intimate with their cigarettes than they ever are with people.

A Step in the Right Direction

When did your relationship with cigarettes change from being friends to being lovers?

A Suggestion

Recall when you first shared intimate moments with your cigarettes. Describe several such moments in your journal. Did you treat your cigarettes like a lover, arranging private rendezvous, turning to them when you were hurt or lonely, trusting your feelings to them completely? What did cigarettes do for you that no human lover could do? Breaking up a love affair is a painful process; are you ready to end *this* love affair? Understanding your relationship with cigarettes and how it changed over the years will help you stay clean and free.

First and Last

Most smokers do not remember much about smoking their first cigarette, usually just the general situation or that it was probably with friends. However, most recovering smokers remember their last cigarette as long as they live. They usually remember the situation ("Super Bowl Sunday, 1984"); many can give the date ("December 31, 1994"), and sometimes even the hour ("Right after dinner on my birthday last year"). This indicates how significant an event quitting smoking was for them. Quitting smoking was an unforgettable milestone in their lives, a moment to celebrate, and an accomplishment to be proud of. Quitting smoking is one of the most significant events in the life of every recovering smoker.

A Step in the Right Direction

When did you smoke your last cigarette? What was happening that day? Why did you select that day? How will you describe that day to your family ten or twenty years from now?

A Suggestion

To help you recall the details of that event many years from now, take a few moments today to record in your journal as much as you can remember about your Quit Day and the events that led up to it. Make your Quit Day an annual celebration of life.

Should You Be Doing More?

Will Rogers once said, "Even if you're on the right track, you'll get run over if you just sit there."

A Step in the Right Direction

Has your recovery been moving along at a steady pace or has it gotten stalled? Are there some parts of your program that are going well, but others that you have neglected? After a number of months clean and free, many recovering smokers start slacking off on their recovery programs, putting themselves at risk for relapse.

A Suggestion

Look closely at each aspect of your recovery program; find the areas in which you could be doing more.

- Have you skipped the occasional page in this book because the questions were too involved or too threatening?
- Have you neglected to contact people you know will be supportive?
- Have you stopped writing your thoughts down in your journal on a regular basis?
- Have you maintained an "attitude of gratitude"?
- Have you started to take your recovery for granted?

What will happen to you if you stop working on your recovery?

Deciding to Quit Smoking Takes Time

Most smokers find it very hard to quit. On average, smokers make three unsuccessful attempts to quit smoking before they succeed. Some smokers are hardly addicted at all; they can usually quit with advice or coercion, or after they have a serious illness. Those who cannot quit so easily have a more serious addiction; the majority of them do not quit until they die. Most current smokers fall into this category—if they could have quit with advice or coercion or after a serious illness, they would have already done so.

A Step in the Right Direction

Was it difficult for you to decide to quit smoking? Many recovering smokers regret their years of smoking and wish they could turn the clock back. You cannot reclaim those years, but you can make your future clean and free. By quitting smoking, you will repair much of the damage. What will you do with the years of life you will gain by quitting smoking now? Have your efforts to quit smoking given you more empathy for smokers who have not been able to quit?

A Suggestion

Share your personal story with a smoker who has not yet decided to quit. It took some time before you finally made the decision to quit, and you had to put out a lot of effort to be successful. You can use these experiences to help a smoker who is still struggling with the decision to quit.

Building Self-Esteem

Many smokers report that their self-esteem has been damaged by their repeated failures to quit smoking. The best way to improve self-esteem is through taking on and meeting challenges, little ones at first, and then bigger ones. Every day, recovering smokers are offered a thousand chances to relapse—by advertisements in magazines and on billboards, by seeing people smoking, by seeing cigarettes for sale, and by smelling other people's cigarette smoke. Each day they live clean and free helps recovering smokers recover some of their self-esteem.

A Step in the Right Direction

Which challenges to your recovery did you triumph over this week? Have you given yourself credit for your success?

A Suggestion

Write a resume of your smokefree week, highlighting various examples of your ability to stay clean and free. Write it as if you were applying for a job as "Smokefree Supervisor." For example:

- "I cleaned out ashtrays in the lunchroom and none of them were mine."
- "I saw a Marlboro billboard and didn't even consider smoking again."
- "I was offered a cigarette and said, 'I don't smoke anymore.'"

How can you apply your success in recovery to other areas of your life?

Desensitize Yourself from Anxiety

Research shows that smokers as a group are no more anxious than nonsmokers. However, quitting smoking makes people *very* anxious. Even *thinking* about quitting is enough to make some smokers run for a cigarette. When smokers first quit, some of their anxiety is due to withdrawal from nicotine; this anxiety can be treated with the nicotine patch. The rest of their anxiety is much harder to deal with. It comes from no longer having a cigarette to help them handle uncomfortable feelings or to rely on in moments of stress.

A Step in the Right Direction

When you were still smoking, did you use cigarettes to help you deal with anxiety? What have you done since you quit smoking to reduce your anxiety?

A Suggestion

Desensitize yourself from anxiety the same way an allergist treats an allergic patient. Start with a situation that only makes you a little bit anxious, like picking someone up at the airport. Instead of medicating your anxiety, allow yourself to experience it, knowing it will pass soon. When the situation is over (and you didn't smoke to relieve the anxiety), review the experience and see what you learned about yourself. Then take on a situation that makes you a bit more anxious, such as working on your income taxes. Keep taking on slightly harder challenges, and eventually you will gain control of your anxiety.

Good News Can Be as Stressful as Bad News

Receiving bad news can be a relapse trigger, but so can receiving good news. Many people are not aware that good news can be as stressful as bad news. Getting an unexpected promotion, winning the lottery, receiving an inheritance, getting a bonus, passing a difficult course, finding something that was lost, resolving a conflict, winning an election—all these good events can be moments of great stress.

A Step in the Right Direction

Your stress level may increase when you get good news, sometimes even more than it would with bad news, and you may want to smoke. Many people want to celebrate when they get good news; they go out, spend some money, have a few drinks, do something that's fun. Which of these activities do you associate with smoking? Many people think only of themselves when they get good news, forgetting that rarely does anyone accomplish great things alone.

A Suggestion

The next time you get good news, ask yourself who helped you achieve your goal. Have you thanked those people for their help? When you think of others (and not just yourself), you will be taking another step toward becoming a better person. How will becoming a better person help you stay clean and free?

The True Colors of Smoking

There are a variety of colors associated with cigarette smoking. Here are a few of them:

- *Red* is the color of a pack of Marlboros.
- *White* is the color of the clean, unblemished paper holding the tobacco.
- *Green* is the color kids turn after they smoke tobacco the first time.
- *Black* is the color of the soot particles deposited in a smoker's lungs with each puff.
- *Yellow* is the color of a smoker's nicotine-stained fingers and nails.
- *Brown* is the color of the stains on the walls, appliances, and furniture in a smoker's home.
- *Pink* is the color of the frothy blood smokers cough up when they get lung disease.
- *Blue* is the color of the anxious face of a chronic lung disease patient, straining to breathe.
- *Gray* is the color of the face of a smoker dying of lung cancer.

A Step in the Right Direction
Now that you have quit smoking, choose something healthy to associate with each of these colors.

A Suggestion
Describe your new color associations in your journal.

Brown and Williamson Tells the Truth

In 1995, the *Journal of the American Medical Association* published seven articles that discussed a group of several thousand internal documents from the Brown and Williamson Company (makers of Kool cigarettes) and its parent company, BAT Industries of the United Kingdom. BAT's various tobacco companies produce about 600 billion cigarettes each year. Dr. John Slade and Dr. Stanton Glantz and their colleagues combed through the documents and found evidence that company scientists knew about the addictive qualities of nicotine in the 1960s. When some of these scientists suggested sharing their research results with Surgeon General Luther Terry (who was working on the 1964 Surgeon General's Report on smoking and health), the company attorney, Addison Yeaman, intervened. In his memo, he stated, "Moreover, nicotine is addictive. . . . We are, then, in the business of selling nicotine, an addictive drug." The research results were never shared with the surgeon general.

A Step in the Right Direction

How do you feel about the efforts of the tobacco companies to suppress the truth about nicotine and tobacco?

A Suggestion

Write to your senators and your congressional representative, telling them how you feel about regulating nicotine.

How Do You Feel about Yourself?

Parents give their children many messages about who they are and what to expect out of life as they grow up. Some children learn that they are loved and appreciated, and that they will be successful; others are frequently told that they are unwanted and undesirable, and that they will never amount to anything. These messages mold children's attitudes about themselves and they mold their expectations. When they become parents, they tend to pass on the same messages to their children.

A Step in the Right Direction

What was your attitude about yourself when you were young, before you started smoking? Did you feel that your parents cared about you and appreciated you? Did you feel "normal"? Many young people feel isolated, rejected, and "abnormal." By learning how to smoke, they immediately become part of a special peer group, and they instantly have a place to belong. Soon, they identify themselves as smokers. Did this happen to you?

A Suggestion

Describe in your journal how becoming a smoker changed your opinion of yourself. Now you have quit smoking. How has quitting smoking changed how you feel about yourself? How will you feel about yourself when you have been clean and free for a year? How could this affect how you treat others?

Freud Could Not Quit Smoking

One of history's most famous smokers was Sigmund Freud, the founder of psychoanalysis. Freud used cocaine to treat his depression, but when he became addicted to cocaine, he quit using it. He also smoked big cigars, often ten a day; one of the most famous pictures of him shows him holding a cigar. Eventually, Freud developed cancer in his mouth and jaw. He tried to quit smoking after he got cancer, but couldn't. He had several surgical operations, but the cancer kept growing and Freud kept on smoking. He finally had to have most of his jaw and part of his face cut away, but he continued to smoke cigars. For many years before his death, he could no longer lecture because his cancer and his surgeries had left his face so badly deformed. He continued to smoke until he died.

A Step in the Right Direction

Freud understood more about the human mind than any of us, yet he was unable to deal with his own nicotine and tobacco dependence. Why do you think he never figured it out? Why could he quit using cocaine but not tobacco? Imagine that you understand more about nicotine and tobacco dependence than Freud did.

A Suggestion

Propose a psychoanalytic explanation for why Freud could not quit smoking and describe your theory in your journal.

Other Dependent Behaviors

In 1950 more than half of Americans smoked; today, only about 25 percent smoke. However, the percentage of smokers among people with other dependencies remains very high. About 75 percent of alcoholics and drug addicts smoke, and about 40 percent of smokers also have a problem with alcohol or other drug dependence.

A Step in the Right Direction

Do you have other dependent behaviors in addition to smoking? This is a good time to look at some of your other behaviors and to ask yourself if you have other dependencies you need to deal with. Examples include alcohol dependence, drug dependence (including marijuana), anorexia or bulimia nervosa, compulsive eating, compulsive spending, compulsive working, compulsive gambling, and compulsive sexual activity. Look carefully at any activity that controls your thoughts or behavior or prevents you from making good choices in your life. Do you have a compulsive behavior that could be a barrier in your life? Are you willing to deal with it as you have dealt with your nicotine and tobacco dependence?

A Suggestion

Ask someone you really trust if he or she thinks you have another dependency to deal with. If you do, will you have the courage to change that behavior too?

What Did Cigarettes Do for You?

Most smokers can report where and when they use cigarettes, but they are not aware of how the cigarettes affect them or why they are using them. After they quit smoking, they are in danger of relapse in situations where they previously relied on cigarettes.

A Step in the Right Direction

What did smoking do for you? Did it help you relax, cope with stress, keep alert, concentrate better, and be sociable? When you are able to identify what smoking did for you, you can find other ways of meeting your needs.

A Suggestion

Look closely at your thoughts and feelings for one day. Take a piece of lined paper and mark it off in half-hour intervals. Every half hour throughout the day, stop and write down the following:

- What situation were you in when you wanted a cigarette?
- What were you thinking and feeling?
- How would a cigarette have changed how you were thinking and feeling?
- What did you do instead of smoking?

This will take three or four minutes each half hour. At the end of the day, review your record and identify clues to how you used cigarettes and situations where you are at greatest risk of relapse. How are you dealing with these threats to your recovery?

Smoking Affects the Smoker's Family

When one person in a family has an addiction, everyone in the family is affected. This is obvious when the drug of addiction is alcohol, heroin, or cocaine. But what if the drug is tobacco? In many families, the smoker disrupts the family in the same way that other addicts do. At first, the family tries to get the smoker to quit by pleading or giving ultimatums. Family members leave smoking cessation literature in prominent places—but the smoker rarely even notices it. Later, after these attempts have failed, family members develop their own form of denial. They make excuses when the smoker goes outside to smoke: "He just stepped out for a minute." They pretend not to notice the smoking: "Oh, I'm used to it." They make excuses for a smoker's illnesses: "Well, there's a lot of flu going around; she just got a bad case." Meanwhile, these family members suffer physically (from the effects of environmental tobacco smoke) and emotionally (feeling powerless, resentful, and frustrated).

A Step in the Right Direction

How did your smoking affect your family? Many recovering smokers never make an effort to find out. Are you willing to?

A Suggestion

Make a list of the ways you think your smoking affected your family. Then ask the members of your family how it affected them, and compare what they tell you with your list.

Smoking Causes Birth Defects

When a pregnant women smokes, chemicals from the cigarette enter her bloodstream and pass through the placenta and into her unborn child. The baby picks up these chemicals even when a nonsmoking pregnant woman breathes environmental tobacco smoke. Some of the most harmful of these chemicals are toxic heavy metals, including cadmium, lead, arsenic, radioactive polonium-210, aluminum, and cobalt. This exposure to heavy metals can lead to spontaneous abortions, damage to the baby's body and brain, and increased risk of crib death (sudden infant death syndrome, or SIDS) in these infants. The risk of SIDS increases even more when the mother is a heavy smoker and when both mother and father smoke. When the mother smokes heavily in the last two weeks of pregnancy, the risk of SIDS is nine times higher than if she never smoked. Quitting smoking anytime during pregnancy helps avoid all these problems, but switching to a low-tar brand does not; low-tar cigarettes are no safer than high-tar cigarettes.

A Step in the Right Direction

Did you ever contribute to an unborn baby absorbing chemicals from tobacco smoke? What do you think now when you see a pregnant woman smoking?

Do You Still Think about Smoking Again?

Some recovering smokers never lose the desire to smoke. They may not be smoking, but they are not in recovery. While their bodies are healthier for not smoking, their minds and spirits still suffer. They have quit smoking, but they are not yet clean and free. They are constantly at a high risk of relapse, because temptations to smoke are everywhere and the tobacco companies are eager to get their old customers back again.

A Step in the Right Direction

Do you still wish you could go back to smoking? Do you imagine that one day you will probably smoke again? If so, you are not yet clean and free. To be clean and free means that your body has been cleansed of toxic smoke and your spirit has been freed from the tyranny of an addicting chemical. When you fully accept that smoking again is no longer an option, the desire to smoke will leave.

A Suggestion

Writing a "Good-bye" letter to tobacco will help you free yourself from tobacco's grip. If you have already written one, pull it out, read it over, and add things that you have learned about yourself in the last month. If you have not written one, start today. Start with "Good-bye Tobacco," and tell tobacco why you have left it behind.

Odor or Aroma?

One of the most common reasons smokers give for deciding to quit smoking is wanting to get rid of the odor of stale cigarette smoke on their breath and clothes. This reason is *serious* enough for them to quit, but it may not be *personal* enough for them to recover.

A Step in the Right Direction

In order to recover—not just quit smoking—you must make your reasons more personal.

A Suggestion

Respond to the following questions in your journal.

- When you were still smoking, did anyone ever tell you that your breath or clothes smelled bad?
- When you take some clothes you haven't worn for a while out of the closet, can you smell the stale smoke on them?
- When you meet smokers, do you ever back off a little because their breath smells so bad? Did your breath smell like that when you were smoking?
- Can you tell that a person is a smoker by the odor on his or her clothing? Did your clothing smell like that when you were smoking?
- Are you proud to be clean and free?

Peer Pressure

Most smokers had their first cigarette when they were teenagers. The average age of smoking initiation is fourteen; 90 percent of current smokers started before they were twenty. Most of these kids got their first cigarette from a friend; peer pressure is the primary reason they started to smoke. For teenagers, acceptance by their peers is more important than just about anything else. At the age of fourteen they are not afraid of getting cancer or heart disease in their fifties or sixties. They can't even conceive of being sixty years old. They know that smoking leads to health problems because they hear about it in school; most kids who smoke say they do not intend to smoke forever—just for a few years. Unfortunately, most of them do continue to smoke, and half of them will smoke until the day they die.

A Step in the Right Direction

Think back to your first few cigarettes. When you started smoking, did you intend to smoke as long as you did? What could a caring adult have done or said to you then that would have prevented you from becoming addicted to nicotine and tobacco? How would this have changed your life?

A Suggestion

Look for an opportunity to help a kid get started on the right path. Contact the smokefree coalition in your area or the American Cancer Society, and volunteer to talk to a group of children about smoking.

Remind Yourself about Recovery

The tobacco companies want their products to be noticed. They write their names on racing cars, advertise on billboards, and give away samples at fairs and sporting events. They like to see actors smoke in the movies so they pay them to smoke on screen. They sell T-shirts, hats, and jackets bearing the names and logos of well-known cigarette brands. They want restaurants and other public places to allow smoking. The tobacco companies know that these constant reminders about smoking influence people who have never smoked to consider smoking, influence current smokers to switch to their brands, and influence recovering smokers to start smoking again.

A Step in the Right Direction

The tobacco companies are not happy that you quit smoking; they were counting on your business for many years to come, and they want you back. They will remind you how much fun it is to smoke and they will try to persuade you that quitting was a stupid thing to do. What can you do to remind yourself about recovery when you see a tobacco company promotion?

A Suggestion

Carry your *Keep Quit* chip with you at all times. When you see something that reminds you about smoking again, touch your chip and remind yourself why you quit smoking. Are you staying focused on recovery?

You Have Been More Successful than Others

Many famous people who relied on their voices for their success were also smokers. John Wayne, Edward R. Murrow, Chet Huntley, Nat King Cole, and Lucille Ball are a few examples. All of these celebrities died prematurely—from lung cancer, caused by their smoking.

A Step in the Right Direction

Did you know that each of these celebrities died from the damage done by their smoking?

- John Wayne was tough and fearless, but he couldn't quit smoking.
- Edward R. Murrow was daring and highly intelligent, but he couldn't quit smoking.
- Chet Huntley was wise and authoritative, but he couldn't quit smoking.
- Nat King Cole was popular and talented, but he couldn't quit smoking.
- Lucille Ball was clever and creative, but she couldn't quit smoking.

Why have you been able to quit smoking when these famous people couldn't?

A Suggestion

Identify the personal characteristics that have helped you successfully quit smoking. In the months and years ahead, you will be at risk of relapse many times. How will you rely on these personal characteristics to help you stay clean and free?

Dealing with Odors as Relapse Triggers

Smokers build up many associations between things they smell and smoking. Some examples include the following:

- The acrid, sulfuric odor of a match
- The sweet, intoxicating smell of a lighter
- The soft, delicate aroma of fresh tobacco
- The heady fragrance of the first billow of smoke from a newly lit cigarette
- The rough, masculine scent of pipe tobacco
- The forlorn smell of old cigarette butts

Each of these smells could be someone's trigger to relapse.

A Step in the Right Direction

Which of those descriptions caught your attention? Which ones brought an image to mind? Which ones made your heart beat a little faster? These smells may be relapse triggers for you. What will you do if a familiar aroma makes you want to start smoking again?

A Suggestion

Those smells all remind you of your romance with cigarettes. They are a threat to your recovery because they remind you of your old lover. How have you ended other relationships? How will you end this one?

Become the Person You Want to Be

Tobacco companies spend billions of dollars each year to create images for their products. They design a different image for each brand in order to appeal to different types of people. Marlboro has the best-known image—the rugged, self-assured, determined cowboy who can take care of himself. Kool promotes an image of being, well, very cool. Virginia Slims promotes an image for women of being thin (*extremely* thin), self-reliant, and independent. Camel used to promote the image of being a mature, sensible man, but the Joe Camel campaign promotes adolescent fantasies (riding motorcycles, dragging girls by their hair, shooting pool, and gambling in Las Vegas).

A Step in the Right Direction

What image attracted you to the brands you used to smoke? What part of that image do you still want to be like? How could this image be a trigger to relapse for you?

A Suggestion

Identify the images the tobacco companies have invented for smokers of the brands you have smoked. Write out a list of these characteristics, and then check off the characteristics that actually describe you. Did smoking create these characteristics, or did you already have them? Now write down the characteristics you would like to have. How can you become more like the person you want to be?

How Will You Deal with Smokers?

Some people are assertive, some are aggressive, and some are passive in their interactions with others. *Assertiveness* is the skill of making sure your own needs are met without intruding on the needs of others. People who are assertive stand up for their own rights. Assertiveness is different from *aggressiveness*. People who are *aggressive* are willing to harm others in order to get their needs met. *Passive* people put other people's needs before their own.

A Step in the Right Direction

Since you quit smoking, have you been assertive in staying away from relapse situations? Many recovering smokers remain passive and do not insist on their right to breathe clean air. Some recovering smokers become aggressive, to the point of ripping cigarettes out of smokers' mouths. What about you?

A Suggestion

Develop your assertiveness skills. This is hard for many people. How assertive have you been?

- Do you prohibit smoking in your home?
- Have you asked your friends who still smoke to not smoke around you?
- Have you suffered in silence while someone smoked in a nonsmoking area?

Start with these three issues and practice becoming more assertive.

What Kind of Recovering Smoker Will You Be?

After people make a significant change, they tend to forget the way they were before. After smokers quit, they often forget how completely cigarettes controlled their lives when they were smoking. As smokers, they vigorously defended their right to smoke; as nonsmokers, their personality and behavior often change quite dramatically.

A Step in the Right Direction

Experience shows that newly recovering smokers usually fall into one of these categories:

- The smug ex-smoker who lets everyone know how he or she quit smoking.
- The aggressive ex-smoker who angrily defends his or her right to breathe clean air.
- The judgmental former smoker who is highly critical of people who still smoke.
- The frightened nonsmoker who is in constant fear of relapse.
- The sympathetic recovering smoker who helps others who are trying to quit.

What kind of recovering smoker will you be?

A Suggestion

Choose one situation you will be in soon that will show what kind of a nonsmoker you are. Predict how you will behave in that situation and write down your prediction in your journal. Afterward, compare what you predicted you would do with what you actually did.

Living with Anxiety

Relapses are common in all addictions, including nicotine and tobacco dependence. When recovering smokers relapse, they are often tense and anxious. Their bodies are loaded with nicotine one minute and craving it the next. They are worried about who will see them smoking, what people will say, and how they will respond. When recovering smokers relapse, they are often so tense that they cannot make reasonable plans for setting a new Quit Day; their anxiety interferes with making good decisions. As the days pass, they rediscover how comforting and available cigarettes can be, and they start depending on them again instead of living with their anxiety and solving their problems.

A Step in the Right Direction

Do you know one or more recovering smokers who have relapsed? Were they extremely anxious after they started smoking again? How could you be of help to a relapsed smoker?

A Suggestion

Show that you understand their fears and their feelings by being patient. When they feel tense and frustrated, they may not be able to see the best strategy for recovery. Recall how tense you were in the first few days after your last cigarette. How long did it take before you calmed down? Sharing your story will give them hope that they can live with their anxiety and set a new Quit Day.

Being a Role Model

Charles Barkley once said that he was a basketball player, not a role model. Whether or not Charles Barkley wanted to be a role model, thousands of youngsters saw him as one. People cannot control whether or not others view them as role models. Young people select their role models from highly visible people who excel at the activities they care about: musicians, movie stars, athletes—and parents—top the list. Some take this situation as a serious responsibility and others don't seem to care.

A Step in the Right Direction

Have you been a role model for a young person? Did your smoking influence that person in any way? Now you are no longer smoking, you have become a role model for others. Your success will inspire others to make an effort to quit smoking.

A Suggestion

Pay attention to the people around you; who is looking up to you as a role model? How will being a role model change your behavior and your life? You may not have wanted to be a role model when you were still smoking; how do you feel about being a role model now that you are clean and free?

What Happened to Yul Brynner?

Yul Brynner, a talented actor, was a heavy smoker all his life and never thought much about his smoking. Like his most famous character, the King of Siam in *The King and I,* he didn't like people telling him what to do. Like the King, he thought nothing would ever happen to him. In his early sixties, however, he was diagnosed with lung cancer. He had surgery, but the cancer had already spread to the rest of his body. After surgery, he made a public service TV ad for the American Cancer Society, which, according to his instructions, was not aired until after he died in 1985. In it, he says, "Now that I'm gone, I tell you: Don't smoke. Whatever you do, just don't smoke. If I could take back that smoking, we wouldn't be talking about my cancer—I'm convinced of that."

A Step in the Right Direction

Would you have had the courage to make an ad like Yul Brynner's if you were dying of lung cancer? After your death, what message would you want to give to the people who care about you?

A Suggestion

Write a one-minute television spot in which you appear after you have died, like Yul Brynner did. What would be your message to those still living? Write your script in your journal so you can come back and read it again.

Bad Days

The support of others improves a recovering smoker's success in avoiding a relapse. Everyone has bad days, but when recovering smokers have bad days, their risk of relapse increases tremendously. At times like these, supportive friends and family can make the difference between staying in recovery and relapsing back to smoking.

A Step in the Right Direction

When you were preparing to quit smoking, you probably identified several people you would ask for help. Have you kept these people updated on your progress? When you tell them about your success, it will make them (and you) feel proud, which will give you even more dedication to your recovery. Who else could you share your progress with? Do you know another recovering smoker you could offer support to? Have you been to a meeting of Nicotine Anonymous, where other recovering smokers seek mutual support?

A Suggestion

Plan to attend a meeting of Nicotine Anonymous on your first anniversary of becoming clean and free. If you have already been to a number of meetings, you understand their value. If you have never been to a Nicotine Anonymous meeting, this is a chance to share your success with others. You can find a meeting in your community by calling the national office at (415) 750-0328.

Whom Did Your Smoking Affect?

When nicotine is in control, smokers do not pay attention to the many people their smoking affects. As nicotine begins to lose control over them, they become aware of how their smoking can harm other people and affect their relationships.

A Step in the Right Direction

At this point in your recovery, nicotine no longer controls your thoughts and feelings. Now you can begin to identify the people your smoking has affected. How did it affect your family and friends? Are you ready to discover how your smoking affected them?

A Suggestion

Take out the list you made of people you may have harmed by your smoking. Rewrite the list in order of how seriously your smoking affected the relationship, from most serious to least serious. Who is at the *bottom* of the list (the least seriously affected)? Make plans to contact that person. Tell him or her about your recovery from nicotine and tobacco dependence, and ask forgiveness for the harm caused by your smoking. Afterward, make some notes in your journal about how you feel. Soon you will be ready to take another name from the list and make amends to that person. Are you willing to make amends to everyone on the list? This is an important step to improve your chances of staying clean and free forever.

Make a Commitment to Recovery

Many smokers are able to quit for a year by *promising* to quit for a year or by *making a bet* with someone. Typically, these people stay clean for exactly a year and then start smoking again. They can *quit smoking* but they start again because they never made a commitment to *recovery.* As a result, nicotine and tobacco dependence continues to control their thoughts, feelings, attitudes, and behavior. They say that they can quit any time, and they can—but they never become truly clean and free because they never make a commitment to recovery.

A Step in the Right Direction

Did you ever make a promise or make a bet to quit smoking for a certain length of time? Why? You have not smoked in some time now; is it because you have quit smoking temporarily or does it mean you have made a commitment to recovery? Your dependence on nicotine and tobacco has not gone away; if you give it a chance, it will take control of your thoughts, feelings, attitudes, and behavior again. How can you prevent this from happening?

A Suggestion

Begin now to plan what you will do to prevent relapse during your *second* year of recovery. Recovery is a lifelong process of growth and of self-awareness—it does not end after one year. Make some notes in your journal about what you intend to do to stay clean and free in the years to come.

Were You Tired of Being Hassled about Smoking?

One of the most common reasons smokers give for deciding to quit smoking is that they get tired of being hassled about their smoking. Once, people smoked everywhere. Today, there are fewer and fewer places where smoking is tolerated. This reason is *serious* enough for them to quit, but it may not be *personal* enough for them to recover.

A Step in the Right Direction

In order to recover—not just quit smoking—you must make your reasons more personal.

A Suggestion

Respond to the following questions in your journal.

- When you were still smoking, did you resent being told you couldn't smoke in certain places? How did you handle your resentment?
- Now that you have quit smoking, what do you do when you see someone smoking in a nonsmoking area?
- What kind of nonsmoker will you be: aggressive or sympathetic, assertive or timid, open or secretive?
- If your child, grandchild, niece, or nephew announced that he or she was going to start smoking, what would you say and do?

Situations Associated with Smoking

Many smokers associate smoking with one or more of these four situations: eating a meal, drinking a cup of coffee, having sex, and driving to work. While these situations are very common associations with smoking, each smoker has his or her unique smoking associations.

A Step in the Right Direction

Which associations with smoking still represent a risk of relapse for you? Here are some to think about:

- Gambling
- Drinking alcohol
- Wanting to lose weight
- Being with other smokers
- Coming to work or leaving work
- Listening to music
- Feeling bored
- Experiencing strong feelings, such as fear, loneliness, or embarrassment

A Suggestion

Use the skills you have developed by reading this book to address each of these associations. Choose one to start with, and do something about it today.

A Daily Responsibility

Relapses are common in all addictions, including nicotine and tobacco dependence. When recovering smokers relapse, they are often highly critical of themselves. They often think their relapse means they are weak or foolish. They may not realize that smoking is an addiction to nicotine and tobacco, not just a bad habit. Their relapse means that the addiction took control of their thoughts, feelings, and actions. If they honestly review their actions, they can usually find where they became careless or lazy in working a recovery program. Staying clean and free does not require intelligence or money or education—but it does require working on recovery every day.

A Step in the Right Direction

Do you know one or more recovering smokers who have relapsed? Did they think they were stupid or weak because of it? Understanding how smoking is a dependence on nicotine and tobacco could help them.

A Suggestion

You can support recovering smokers in relapse by helping them understand how their smoking is an addiction, not a bad habit. When they understand this, they will be able to work on recovery instead of wasting their energy fighting the urge to smoke. What evidence would you use to show someone how nicotine and tobacco dependence is an addiction?

All Relapses Are Serious

Some recovering smokers who relapse use the word "slip" to imply that relapses are not important—just little things, nothing to worry about. Research shows, however, that a recovering smoker who takes a single puff from a cigarette has a 95 percent chance of being a regular smoker six months later. Each relapse exacts a price—in deteriorating health, in loss of self-esteem, and in the shame recovering smokers experience when they have to admit they are smoking again. They may become depressed, which can make them physically ill. Their self-confidence may fall so far that they never make another effort to quit smoking.

A Step in the Right Direction

Did you once think that a slip was different from a relapse? Did you believe that slips were insignificant and that most recovering smokers who slip are able to get clean and free again? Research shows otherwise; most recovering smokers who smoke a single cigarette return to regular daily smoking, and most of them continue to smoke until they die. "Slip" could also stand for "Smoking Levies Its Price."

A Suggestion

Imagine what would happen if you were to start smoking again today. What would be the price to you in terms of health, self-esteem, and self-confidence? Make some notes in your journal about the price you would pay if you relapsed today.

Identify Personal Reasons for Staying Clean and Free

It is not hard to identify *logical* reasons to quit smoking, such as to stay healthy, to save money, and to avoid damaging property. Everyone knows these reasons, but they are rarely enough to convince a smoker to quit. In order to quit, smokers have to turn their logical reasons into *personal reasons.* Recovering smokers also have logical reasons to stay clean and free, but they must make their reasons personal. Logical reasons alone are not sufficient to ensure a smokefree future.

A Step in the Right Direction

Now that you have quit smoking, your challenge is to stay clean and free. You certainly have many logical reasons for not wanting to relapse, but do you have personal reasons? Look back at the *personal* reasons you have identified for wanting to quit; you recorded some of them in your journal. What do you think of these reasons today?

A Suggestion

Take each reason and update it, making it more personal and more specific to your current situation. You can use both logical reasons and personal reasons to improve the quality of your recovery: use your logical reasons to explain why you have quit smoking to others; use your personal reasons to explain why you have quit smoking *to yourself.*

Facing the Truth Can Be Painful

Smokers avoid facing the truth. They have been polluting their lungs, damaging their arteries, and filling their bodies with toxic chemicals for years—and they burn up $1,000 to $2,000 each year to do so. They make excuses for their illness, refuse to listen to the advice of friends and family, reject the suggestions of doctors, defend their cigarettes, and keep on smoking. This is known as *denial,* the unconscious resistance to accepting the truth. Smokers in denial stay insulated from reality, but the damage to their bodies continues. Only when faced with obvious and painful evidence of the damage caused by smoking are they able to break through their denial. For many, it is too late.

A Step in the Right Direction

Can you recall some examples of your denial? When did you finally accept your nicotine and tobacco dependence? Only when the pain of your smoking exceeded the pleasure of it were you able to accept the truth and move on. How can you be sure you are completely free of denial?

A Suggestion

Reach out to a recovering smoker who is not as far along in recovery as you are. In telling your story to another recovering smoker, you will be able to tell if traces of denial remain in your thinking. Helping another recovering smoker will help both of you stay clean and free.

Confronting Your Fears

You gain experience, courage and confidence by every experience in which you really stop to look fear in the face. You are able to say to yourself, "I lived through this horror. I can take the next thing that comes along."... You must do the thing you think you cannot do.

—ELEANOR ROOSEVELT
You Learn by Living

A Step in the Right Direction

When you first thought about quitting smoking, were you afraid? Did you think you would fail? Many smokers are so afraid of failure that they never try to quit smoking. What event finally convinced you to confront your fears? Many recovering smokers say that quitting smoking was the hardest thing they ever did, and that their confidence in themselves increased as a result. Has your self-confidence already increased? Imagine how you will feel about yourself when you have been clean and free for a year.

A Suggestion

Write a few lines in your journal about what you fear the most about quitting smoking. Review what you wrote in a month or two; you will discover that you have triumphed over your fear, which will empower you to take on your next challenge.

Take Credit for Your Success

People frequently look down the road at the many miles they have yet to travel and say, "It's too far. I'll never make it." They rarely take the time to look behind them and appreciate the distance they have traveled and say, "Look how far I've come!" A journey of recovery is like that—recovering smokers always have further to go, but they need to give themselves credit for making the decision to quit, for surviving nicotine withdrawal, and for triumphing in a variety of relapse situations.

A Step in the Right Direction

How far have you come on your journey of recovery? Have you paused to give yourself credit for the progress you have made?

A Suggestion

Make a list of your accomplishments so far. Consider these four:

1. It has been ___ days since I smoked my last cigarette.
2. Because I quit smoking, I have not smoked ___ cigarettes I otherwise would have smoked.
3. I have saved $___ because I quit smoking.
4. I have successfully resisted the urge to smoke ___ times in the last week.

Today is a day to give yourself credit for your many successes.

Live in the Present

Some people live their lives in the past, regretting their mistakes, holding on to resentments, and forever wishing that things had been different. Some people live their lives for the future, hoping things will get better, promising their loved ones that they will change, and praying for their problems to be solved. Neither living in the past nor living for the future helps smokers quit smoking. Those who successfully quit smoking are the ones who accept the past and plan for the future, but live each day in the present.

A Step in the Right Direction

Do you regret the years you spent smoking? Do you worry about having shortened your life? These are examples of living in the past. The past is gone and there is no way to change it. Do you wish for the day when your craving for a cigarette will end or hope the day will come when your life will get back to normal? Do you put off making changes because the time isn't right or because there will be less stress later? These are examples of living in the future. The future isn't here yet, and no one knows what it will bring. You can only do something about the present.

A Suggestion

In your journal, list some of the things you are doing *in the present* to improve your chances of staying clean and free forever.

Did Nicotine Hide Your Anger?

All mind- and mood-altering chemicals (including nicotine) tend to dampen the intensity of anger. Alcoholics do this with alcohol, cocaine addicts do it with cocaine, heroin addicts do it with heroin, and smokers do it with nicotine. Nicotine keeps smokers out of touch with their feelings. When they are angry and then smoke, their awareness of being angry goes away—but the anger and the situation that caused it remain. After quitting, recovering smokers are often amazed to discover how angry they are.

A Step in the Right Direction

How do you deal with anger?

- Do you usually deal with anger when it arises?
- Do you usually stuff your anger and put off dealing with it?
- Do you lash out at everybody when you are angry?
- Do you get headaches, back pain, or stomach pains when you are angry?

Many people (not just smokers) do not know how to focus their anger where it belongs. To stay clean and free, you will have to learn how to deal with your anger without using nicotine.

A Suggestion

In *The Angry Book,* by Theodore Rubin, you will find lots of good information to help you understand your anger better.

Cigarettes Became a Part of You

Smokers develop a special relationship with their cigarettes. At first, cigarettes are companions, accompanying smokers wherever they go. Soon, they become friends that smokers share good times with. Later, cigarettes become a smoker's best friend, the one to rely on in times of trouble. In time, cigarettes become a smoker's lover, and they share intimate moments together. For many smokers, cigarettes eventually become just like a part of their body, like a hand or a finger. They no longer think of a cigarette as a *thing;* it becomes part of them. This makes quitting very difficult, because quitting smoking feels like tearing off a part of their body.

A Step in the Right Direction

When you were still smoking, did you feel more natural with a cigarette between your fingers than without one? Could you light and smoke a cigarette without thinking about it, while doing something else?

A Suggestion

Recall when you first treated your cigarette as an extension of your hand. Your relationship with cigarettes has progressed from companion, to friend, to best friend, to lover, and finally to an extension of yourself. No wonder quitting smoking is such a challenge. Understanding your relationship with cigarettes and how it changed over the years will help you stay clean and free.

Resentments Are a Threat to Your Recovery

People get resentful when they feel that they are being treated unfairly or that others are getting more than they deserve. Holding on to resentments is one way that people prove to themselves that they are right—if they gave up their resentments, they would have to admit that they could be wrong. When people think about how they were wronged, they seethe with anger They grit their teeth, bite their nails, twist their jaws, and clench their fists. They want satisfaction; they want relief. When recovering smokers feel this way, they sometimes grab a cigarette and smoke it, trying to control their feelings. When this happens, they usually return to regular daily smoking.

A Step in the Right Direction

Are you holding on to resentments? When you are reminded of your resentments, do you think about smoking again? A cigarette might make you feel better temporarily, but a cigarette will not solve your problems—only *you* can do that.

A Suggestion

Let go of your resentments to improve your chances of staying clean and free. A person who *quits smoking* learns to not use cigarettes to solve problems. A person in *recovery* discovers how to become a better person. How will letting go of your resentments help you become a better person?

Do You Like Yourself Better as a Nonsmoker?

Recovering smokers are often tempted to smoke when a smoker offers them a cigarette. Many smokers feel guilty about their smoking and don't want to be reminded that they could quit if they made a serious effort. They try—consciously or unconsciously—to get former smokers to start smoking again by projecting their guilty feelings on to them. After all, if everyone smoked, they wouldn't have to think about quitting.

A Step in the Right Direction

One day someone may try to get you to smoke again, saying, "You know—you've changed. I liked you much better when you smoked." Your recovery is a constant reminder to guilty smokers that they have not been able to do what you have done. Because *they* feel guilty, they will try to make *you* feel guilty; it's easier to tempt you to start smoking again than it is for them to quit. If someone tries to make you feel guilty because you quit smoking, how will you respond?

A Suggestion

Consider saying, "*You* may not like me as well, but *I* like myself a lot better now that I'm clean and free." What other good responses have you thought of?

Intimacy

Smokers become intimate with their cigarettes. In many ways, they become more intimate with their cigarettes than they ever become with other people. Intimacy does not mean sex: it means sharing openly and honestly with another the truth about oneself. Intimacy means taking down the defenses that set people apart and make them feel isolated.

A Step in the Right Direction

Did you become intimate with your cigarettes? Recall a time when you were still smoking and got bad news—*really* bad news. Did you immediately think of sharing your fear, your pain, your sadness, and your hurt with another person, or did you think first about smoking a cigarette? Most smokers reluctantly admit that they usually smoked a cigarette before doing anything else. Did you? If so, did it make you feel even closer to your cigarettes? Since you no longer smoke, you no longer have cigarettes to depend on. Since you quit smoking, what is the worst news you have received? Did you think about smoking? What did you do instead of smoking?

A Suggestion

Devote some time today to nurturing the intimacy between you and another person. To stay clean and free, you will have to learn how to trust other people with the truth of your life. Where would you like to start?

Don't Let Up Now

Recovering from nicotine and tobacco dependence is an all-day, everyday challenge for every recovering smoker. At first, *just not smoking* takes a lot of energy; as the weeks and months pass, however, the intense desire to smoke fades. At that point, many recovering smokers get bored with the day-to-day necessity of working on recovery and they stop moving forward. They lose interest in examining their thoughts, feelings, attitudes, and behaviors. They become comfortable, and then they become complacent—and then, many relapse.

A Step in the Right Direction

Have you lost interest in working on your recovery? You have been clean and free for some time now. As the challenge of *just not smoking* fades, have you stopped working on your recovery every day?

A Suggestion

Continue to work on your recovery every day. This book was designed to make it easier for you to do so. Now that you are nearing the end of the book, begin using the index to pick out subjects that you want to work on. Review what you have written in your journal, and reach out to newly recovering smokers. Are you willing to make a commitment to work on your recovery each and every day?

What Did You Give Up? What Did You Gain?

When smokers think about quitting, they usually think first about what they will have to *give up* when they quit smoking and only later realize what they will *gain* by quitting. Who can blame them? Smoking has been an integral part of their lives for ten or twenty or even thirty years; they have associated smoking a cigarette with just about everything they do. They know what they will miss; they can only guess what they will gain.

A Step in the Right Direction

When you were getting ready to quit smoking, what did you think you would miss most? What do you miss most about smoking today? Since you are no longer smoking, you have proved that you can successfully deal with life without cigarettes.

A Suggestion

Make a list in your journal of the things you miss most about smoking. After each item, write down what you have done to replace that aspect of smoking in your life. Then consider what you have gained by quitting smoking. What do you expect to gain in the next month? The next year? You can use your experience to help someone who is still afraid to quit. Seek out a person who is still struggling with the decision to quit smoking and share how you survived the losses and how you have benefited from living clean and free.

Major Depression Is a Real Disease

Many smokers say they feel depressed after they quit smoking. "Feeling blue" or "feeling crummy" is different from the emotional disorder doctors call "major depressive episode." The symptoms of major depression include crying spells, withdrawing from activities, a big change in sleep patterns or appetite, thoughts of suicide or self-harm, feelings of being worthless or hopeless, and loss of interest in recreation. Depressive episodes usually last days or weeks at a time; mood swings that take place within one day or over a few hours do not meet the criteria for major depression. Major depression is a real disease, just like diabetes. Diabetics have a chemical imbalance in the pancreas that affects their blood sugar; people with major depression have a chemical imbalance in the brain that affects their thinking, their mood, and their behavior.

A Step in the Right Direction

Many of the symptoms of major depression are also seen in nicotine withdrawal—but your nicotine withdrawal symptoms went away a long time ago.

A Suggestion

If you have had several symptoms of major depression, ask for an evaluation by a counselor, therapist, psychiatrist, or family doctor. If you meet the criteria for major depression, you will feel a lot better with proper treatment.

Complete Your "Good-bye Tobacco" Letter

Research shows that out of every one hundred smokers, eighty-five say they wish they could quit. Twenty say they intend to quit within a year, but only seven actually do, and only one or two of them stay quit for a year. People who want to be successful must do everything in their power to be among the small group of long-term recovering smokers.

A Step in the Right Direction

How long did you smoke before you said, "I'd like to quit smoking"? When did you first say, "I intend to quit within a year"? Did you do it? How long did you stay quit that time? Most smokers make several unsuccessful quit attempts before they are successful—the average is three.

A Suggestion

You can improve your chances of making *this* effort successful by writing a "Good-bye" letter to tobacco. If you have already written one, pull it out, read it over, and add things that you have learned over the last month. If you have not written one, start today. Start with "Good-bye Tobacco," and tell tobacco why you have left it behind. Complete your "Good-bye Tobacco" letter and read it to someone you trust. This will be an important moment on your journey of recovery, one you will remember for years. Keep your letter in a safe place and read it again on the anniversary of your last cigarette.

Which People Are Still Relapse Triggers for You?

Seeing certain people can be relapse triggers for recovering smokers.

A Step in the Right Direction

Are there some people you just don't get along with? Take a few moments to complete these sentences:

- I feel angry when I see _____.
- I feel resentful when I see _____.
- I feel defiant when I see _____.
- I feel intimidated when I see _____.
- I feel guilty when I see _____.

Just seeing one of these people could make you want to smoke again because they bring up strong feelings in you that you may not fully understand. Who might be a relapse trigger for you?

A Suggestion

Pay attention to your feelings as you go through the day. Identify how you feel with each person you meet or speak to. Then complete the above sentences in your journal with as many names as you can think of. Add more sentences, too, if you like. Whenever you see someone who brings up strong feelings in you and you think about smoking again, ask yourself, "If I start smoking again, who will suffer—that person, or me?"

What Are Your New Plans?

Some children grow up believing that the world is a beautiful place, full of opportunity; others see it as a frightening place, full of danger. They learn these attitudes about life from their personal experiences and from what they are told by their parents, teachers, other adults, and peers. Some children learn that cigarettes are symbols of adulthood and that smokers are leaders; others learn that cigarettes are unsafe and that smokers are foolish. These attitudes influence their decision to smoke or not to smoke. Psychologists report that attitudes that have been ingrained since childhood may never change and that children who develop positive attitudes about smoking usually carry these attitudes into adulthood.

A Step in the Right Direction

What were your attitudes about the future before you started smoking? Did you expect to be a success or a failure? How did becoming a smoker change your attitudes about the future?

A Suggestion

Describe in your journal how quitting smoking has changed your attitudes about the future. By quitting smoking, you have added five to fifteen years to your life. What will you do in those extra years? What plans are you making for the future that you could not have made before you quit smoking?

Were You Embarrassed about Smoking?

One of the most common reasons smokers give for deciding to quit smoking is that they are embarrassed about their smoking. This reason is *serious* enough for them to quit, but it may not be *personal* enough for them to recover.

A Step in the Right Direction

In order to recover—not just quit smoking—you must make your reasons more personal.

A Suggestion

Respond to the following questions in your journal.

- When you first started smoking, were you proud to be a smoker?
- When was the first time you recall being embarrassed that you were still smoking?
- Did you ever lie to someone about having smoked because you were too embarrassed to admit you were still smoking?
- Did you ever hide the evidence of having smoked so it would look as if you had already quit smoking?
- Has a child ever embarrassed you by asking you to quit smoking?
- Are you embarrassed when you see old pictures of yourself with a cigarette?
- Are you proud to be clean and free?

Are You Willing to Accept Support?

Relapses are common in all addictions, including nicotine and tobacco dependence. Since most smokers make several serious attempts at quitting before succeeding, they are quite familiar with relapse by the time they finally succeed at staying clean and free. Relapsed smokers often feel ashamed and embarrassed; they isolate themselves because they don't want to deal with their relapse. Even though they know that many smokers relapse after quitting, they still feel as if they are the only ones who ever did such a foolish thing.

A Step in the Right Direction

Do you know one or more recovering smokers who have relapsed? What could you do to support and encourage them? Support from recovering smokers greatly improves a smoker's chances of quitting successfully. However, many relapsed smokers are unwilling to accept help from others; they put a lot of pressure on themselves to succeed and insist on doing it alone. What could you do to encourage people like this to accept help?

A Suggestion

Tell them what it was like for you to have to face things you don't like about yourself. Was it worth it in the long run? Hearing about your personal experience will make it easier for them to deal with their relapse. And sharing your experience with others will help you understand your own addiction even better.

Why Did You Quit Smoking?

Some recovering smokers get angry at themselves for waiting so long to quit. They often feel foolish for having smoked for ten or twenty or even thirty years. If they are the last of their friends to quit smoking, they may feel humiliated because it took them so long to take action. When they were smoking, they used their cigarettes to help them feel better when they felt ashamed; as recovering smokers, they have to learn how to deal with strong feelings without their favorite chemical.

A Step in the Right Direction

Did you ever feel foolish because you smoked for as long as you did? Did most of your friends quit smoking before you did? What was it like to be one of the last smokers among your friends? Fortunately, you quit before it was too late, and now you can be proud of your success. Have you taken pride in your accomplishment?

A Suggestion

In your journal, make a short list of what you have already gained by quitting smoking. Then make a list of what you expect to gain in the next five years by staying clean and free. Any single item on your list, by itself, would be reason enough to quit smoking. How about all of them taken together?

Living According to Your Personal Values

Each person holds certain moral values as being important to them. Most people rate *honesty, abiding by the law, taking care of one's body,* and *being a role model for others* as important moral values. It's not easy to live according to these values and do the right thing all the time. Trying to earn a living, having to get along with others, dealing with "the system," needing to be comforted, and seeing other people get more than they deserve tempt the average person to lie (a little), to cheat (a little), to take a little extra, or to break the law (just a little). The rewards of yielding to temptation are immediate and tangible; the rewards for doing the right thing are not always apparent.

A Step in the Right Direction

Do you rate these four moral values as important in your own life? Do you do a good job of holding to them?

A Suggestion

Write down some of your own moral values (including these four, if you believe in them). How was smoking a violation of your moral values? By staying clean and free, how will you be demonstrating a new commitment to your values?

Dealing with Painful Memories

Many recovering smokers survive every temptation to smoke until they begin dealing with a painful memory. When they recall their personal history of abuse, loss, failure, or embarrassment, they want a cigarette. When they were smoking, they used the nicotine in cigarettes like a narcotic to suppress the memories; without this drug, the painful memories return. If they have not learned other ways of dealing with the feelings these memories cause, they often return to smoking.

A Step in the Right Direction

Everyone has unhappy memories from the past. When you were still smoking, did you use cigarettes to help you suppress yours? Now that you are no longer smoking, these memories may return. Smoking a cigarette never resolved your pain; it just helped you avoid dealing with it. Now how will you deal with the pain these memories cause? Have you been tempted to return to smoking to suppress your memories?

A Suggestion

Don't try to deal with these painful memories on your own; if you do, you are putting yourself at a very high risk of relapse. It is much safer to ask for help and support from a friend, a family member, or a counseling professional. Whom do you trust enough to share your painful memories with?

Understanding Your Relationship with Tobacco

After many years of smoking, smokers eventually come to look on their cigarettes as if they are a part of their bodies. For a dedicated smoker struggling with the decision to quit, giving up cigarettes often feels like ripping off a finger or a foot or an ear. Smokers need some time to get used to the idea of surrendering a part of themselves. Because this is so hard to accept, more than half of all smokers don't quit until the day they die.

A Step in the Right Direction

To stay clean and free, you will have to do more than just no-smoke—you will also have to understand your unique relationship with tobacco. Have you devoted time to understanding this relationship? Were you so addicted to cigarettes that they became a part of you?

A Suggestion

Imagine being completely healthy until one day when you discover a tumor in your arm, and it is diagnosed as a highly malignant cancer. Would it take some time to accept having your arm amputated, even though it would save your life? Cigarettes became as much a part of you as your arm—you worked with them, played with them, took them everywhere, and used them in dozens of ways every day. But you eventually accepted that cigarettes were threatening your life, and you decided to quit smoking. Have you finally accepted that you can never smoke again?

Guided Imagery Can Help You Stay Clean and Free

Guided imagery is a technique of focusing the power of the mind on a problem in the body. Using guided imagery, recovering smokers can put their bodies into a state of deep relaxation while their minds are in a state of intense concentration. Usually used to combat anxiety and insomnia, guided imagery has also been used by cancer patients to attack their tumors, by tuberculosis patients to subdue tuberculosis germs, and by patients with spinal cord damage to repair their injuries.

A Step in the Right Direction

If guided imagery can help these people, it can also help you repair the damage done by smoking and improve your chances of recovery. Are you willing to do whatever it takes to stay clean and free?

A Suggestion

Use the guided imagery exercises you have learned by reading this book every day; you will feel more relaxed and your general health will improve. To learn more about guided imagery, read books by Bernie Siegel and Carl Simonton. Audiotapes about guided imagery are available at most bookstores; you can even make your own guided imagery tape, complete with sound effects. Use guided imagery to help you deal with anxiety, to get to sleep at night, and to help your body repair the damage done by smoking.

Making Amends Is Another Step in Recovery

One of the hardest things about becoming a better person is being honest about the consequences of old behaviors. One of the unintended consequences of smoking is that nonsmokers can be harmed by other people's smoking.

A Step in the Right Direction

Whom did you harm directly by smoking (because of the smoke from your cigarettes)? Whom did your smoking affect in other ways (by not being available, by spending your money on tobacco, by choosing to spend your time with a cigarette instead of with someone you care about)? Are you prepared to make amends to the people whose lives you may have harmed by your smoking?

A Suggestion

Return to your list of people you may have harmed by your smoking. Has the time come to make amends to others on the list? Have you planned to complete these amends? Many recovering smokers identify fear, embarrassment, shame, and low self-esteem as barriers to making amends. Keep in mind that the goal of making amends is to make a clean break with smoking so that you improve the quality of your life as a recovering smoker. While making amends will certainly help the people on your list feel better, the primary reason for making amends is to make *you* feel better. You are making amends to ensure that *you* stay clean and free.

Congratulations Again

You have come to the end of *Keep Quit!* You once thought that *stopping smoking* was a reasonable goal; you soon realized that when smokers stop smoking, they fully intend to start smoking again. Later, you set *quitting smoking* as your goal; you made a commitment to not start smoking again. Now you have made *recovery* your goal; you no longer see yourself as a smoker and smoking again is not an option for you. Recovery, however, is a process, not an endpoint; recovery is the journey, not the destination. Each day that you live is another day on this journey. Along the way, you will discover much about nicotine and tobacco dependence and much more about yourself. You may feel strongly about how the world should change. Having quit smoking, you will be better prepared to assert yourself in the world and work toward these changes. Gandhi once wrote, "You must be the change you wish to see in the world." By working with this program, you have shown that you can accomplish these goals.

A Suggestion

Continue to use this book to help further your progress in recovery. Review pages that were significant to you; use the index to look up specific subjects or to help you solve problems. And most important of all, review what you have written in your journal—it is the chronicle of your recovery.

Bibliography

Brigham, J., J.E. Henningfield, and M.L. Stitzer. 1990. Smoking relapse: A review. *International Journal of the Addictions* 25:1239–55.

A review of factors that predict relapse in people who have quit smoking.

Cook, D.G., P.H. Whincup, M.J. Jarvis, D.P. Strachan, O. Papacosta, and A. Bryant. 1994. Passive exposure to tobacco smoke in children aged five to seven years: Individual, family, and community factors. *British Medical Journal* 308:384–89.

Children absorb significant amounts of nicotine from parents' smoking.

DiClemente, C.C., J.O. Prochaska, S.K. Fairhurst, W.F. Velicer, M.M. Velasquez, and J.S. Rossi. 1991. The process of smoking cessation: An analysis of precontemplation, contemplation, and preparation stages of change. *Journal of Consulting and Clinical Psychology* 59:295–304.

Smokers move along a continuum of change: precontemplation, contemplation, determination (preparation), action, maintenance . . . and (frequently) relapse. They may remain in relapse, or may re-enter contemplation.

DiFranza, J.R., J.W. Richards, P.M. Paulman, N. Wolf-Gillespie, C. Fletcher, R.D. Jaffe, and D. Murray. 1991. RJR-Nabisco's cartoon camel promotes Camel cigarettes to children. *Journal of the American Medical Association* 266:3149–53.

Camel cigarettes increased the market share among children from 0.5 percent to 32.8 percent after the Joe Camel promotion began in 1988.

Ferguson, T. 1988. *The no-nag, no-guilt, do-it-your-own-way guide to quitting smoking.* New York: Ballantine.

Offers a wide variety of helpful suggestions for people who are in early action stage of quitting.

Fischer, P.M., M.P. Schwartz, J.W. Richards, A.O. Goldstein, and T.H. Rojas. 1991. Brand logo recognition by children aged three to six years: Mickey Mouse and Old Joe the Camel. *Journal of the American Medical Association* 266:3145–48.

Nearly as many six-year-olds recognize Joe Camel as recognize Mickey Mouse (91 percent versus 100 percent).

Glassman, A.H. 1993. Cigarette smoking: Implications for psychiatric illness. *American Journal of Psychiatry* 150:546–53.

Depression and nicotine/tobacco dependence are linked.

Heatherton, T.F., L.T. Kozlowski, R.C. Frecker, and K.O. Fagerström. 1991. The Fagerström Test for Nicotine Dependence: A revision of the Fagerström Tolerance Questionnaire. *British Journal of Addictions* 86:1119–27.

The Fagerström Test for Nicotine Dependence correlates with cotinine levels.

Henningfield, J.E., and R.M. Keenan. 1993. Nicotine delivery kinetics and abuse liability. *Journal of Consulting and Clinical Psychology* 61:743–50.

Review of addictive properties of nicotine.

Hurt, R.D., L.C. Dale, P.A. Fredrickson, C.C. Caldwell, G.A. Lee, K.P. Offord, G.G. Lauger, Z. Marusic, L.W. Neese, and T.G. Lundber. 1994. Nicotine patch therapy for smoking cessation combined with physician advice and nurse follow-up. *Journal of the American Medical Association* 271:595–600.

Nicotine patch doubles quit rate at one year in an intensive smoking cessation program.

Kottke, T.E., R.N. Battista, G.H. DeFriese, and M.L. Brekke. 1988. Attributes of successful smoking cessation interventions in medical practice: A meta-analysis of thirty-nine controlled trials. *Journal of the American Medical Association* 259:2883–89.

Meta-analysis of 39 studies: 50 percent relapse after one week; 88 percent relapse by one year.

Mulligan, S.C., J.G. Masterson, J.G. Devane, and J.G. Kelly. 1990. Clinical and pharmacokinetic properties of a transdermal nicotine patch. *Clinical Pharmacology and Therapeutics* 47:331–37.

Nicotine patch produces steady-state nicotine levels in the range of 10–20 ng/ml.

Orleans, C.T., N. Resch, E. Noll, M.K. Keintz, B.K. Rimer, T.V. Brown, and T.M. Snedden. 1994. Use of transdermal nicotine in a state-level prescription plan for the elderly. *Journal of the American Medical Association* 271:601–7.

Patch plus ten minutes physician counseling doubles quit rate of the patch without counseling.

Perkins, K.A., L.H. Epstein, B.L. Marks, R.L. Stiller, and R.G. Jacob. 1989. The effect of nicotine on energy expenditure during light physical activity. *New England Journal of Medicine* 320:898–903.

BMR drops when smokers quit: 5 percent at rest and 12 percent during exercise.

Pomerleau, O.F., C.S. Pomerleau, E.M. Morrell, and J.M. Lownbergh. 1991. Effects of fluoxetine on weight gain and food intake in smokers who reduce nicotine intake. *Psychoneuroendocrinology* 16:433–40.

Giving Prozac prevents weight gain when smokers quit.

Reynolds, P., and T. Shachtman. 1989. *The gilded leaf: Triumph, tragedy and tobacco.* Boston: Little, Brown and Co.

The story of the Reynolds family and the R. J. Reynolds Tobacco Company as told by the grandson of the founder.

Sachs, D. 1986. Cigarette smoking: Health effects and cessation strategies. *Clinics in Geriatric Medicine* 2:337–62.

Extensive review of the benefits of smoking cessation.

Shipley, R. 1990. *QuitSmart: A guide to freedom from cigarettes.* Durham, N.C.: JB Press.

A well-researched cognitive-behavioral approach to quitting smoking.

Transdermal Nicotine Study Group. 1991. Transdermal nicotine for smoking cessation: Six-month results from two multicenter controlled clinical trials. *Journal of the American Medical Association* 266:3133–48.

Nicotine patch doubles quit rate at twenty-four weeks.

U.S. Department of Health and Human Services. 1988. *The health consequences of smoking: Nicotine addiction.* Washington, D.C.: U.S. Department of Health and Human Services, Public Health Service, Office of Smoking and Health (DHHS Publication 88–8406).

Extensively documented evaluation of the addicting qualities of nicotine.

———. 1990. *The health benefits of smoking cessation: A report of the Surgeon General.* Rockville, Md.: U.S. Department of Health and Human Services, Public Health Service, Office of Smoking and Health.

Important surgeon general's report that documents the value of smoking cessation.

U.S. Environmental Protection Agency. 1992. *Respiratory health effects of passive smoking: Lung cancer and other disorders.* Washington, D.C.: U.S. Environmental Protection Agency, Office of Health and Environmental Assessment, EPA Publication (EPA/600/6–90/006F).

Extensive documentation of the damage caused by environmental tobacco smoke.

Index

About the Author

Terry A. Rustin, M.D., specializes in addiction medicine. He is assistant professor at the University of Texas Medical School at Houston, and he serves as the medical director of the Addiction Treatment Program at the Harris County Psychiatric Center. Dr. Rustin is a certified psychodrama therapist and trainer, and is director of Rediscovery: the Psychodrama Institute of the Southwest.

Dr. Rustin has had a special interest in the treatment of nicotine and tobacco dependence since 1979, when he ran his first treatment group—a complete failure. Since then, he has developed a variety of successful strategies for treating nicotine and tobacco dependence and for incorporating its treatment into chemical dependency treatment programs.

For price and order information, or a free catalog,
please call our Telephone Representatives

HAZELDEN

1-800-328-9000   **1-651-213-4000**   **1-651-213-4590**
(Toll-Free. U.S., Canada,   (Outside the U.S.   (24-Hour FAX)
and the Virgin Islands)   and Canada)

http://www.Hazelden.org
(World Wide Web site on the Internet)

Pleasant Valley Road • P.O. Box 176 • Center City, MN 55012-0176